How to Succeed in the Cannabis Industry, 3rd Ed.

© **The WeedHead™ & Company All rights reserved.**

Protected by the copyright laws of the United States and international treaties.

No part of this publication in whole or in part may be copied, duplicated, reproduced or transmitted in any form or by any means, electronic or mechanical, including photocopying, recording, or by any information storage and retrieval system, without the express written permission from the publisher.

Copyright and other intellectual property laws protect these materials and any unauthorized reproduction or retransmission will constitute an infringement of copyright law.

Federal law provides severe civil and criminal penalties for the unauthorized reproduction, distribution, or exhibition of copyrighted materials. Penalties for criminal and statutory copyright infringement are set forth at 18 U.S.C. § 2319.

This material has been written and published for educational purposes. For information about this title or to order other books and electronic media, please contact the publisher.

Published By The WeedHead™ & Company, 54 Belle La Blanc, Las Vegas, NV 89123

info@theweedhead.com

www.theweedhead.com

3rd Edition, October 2019

ISBN: 978-0-578-22356-8 (Softcover, Print)

Printed in the United States of America.

TABLE OF CONTENTS:
How to Succeed in the Cannabis Industry

FOREWORD by Roz McCarthy, CEO of Minorities for Medical Marijuana	1
INTRODUCTION: How to Use this Workbook	5
TARGET TO THC: Crossing over to Cannabis	11
PART 1: ROLES IN THE LEGAL CANNABIS INDUSTRY	**17**
CULTIVATOR / FARMER	19
PARALLELS IN HISTORY: California Gold Rush	22
OPPORTUNITIES IN CANNABIS: The "Picks & Shovels" Mindset	27
TOP ROLES IN CANNABIS	32
PART 1: KEY TAKEAWAYS	35
PART 2: SECTORS IN THE LEGAL CANNABIS INDUSTRY	**41**
GENETICS	42
Seeds	43
Clones	43
Tissue Cultures	44
CULTIVATION	48
Nursery	50
Sun Grown	52
Lamp Grown	52
Organic	54
PROCESSING & MANUFACTURING	57
Extraction	64
Infusion	66
Formulation	75
Delivery Mechanisms	77
HEMP: CBD PRODUCTS & MORE	82
VETERINARY & PETS	91
PACKAGING	94
SOFTWARE & INFORMATION TECHNOLOGY	99
MARKETING	102
Event Marketing	104
Content Marketing	105
Influencer Marketing	107
SALES & DISTRIBUTION	111
RETAIL	116
TOURISM	119
EVENTS	122
REAL ESTATE	125
INSURANCE	128
HUMAN RESOURCES	130
LEGAL	132
EDUCATION	134
PART 2: KEY TAKEAWAYS	137
CONCLUSION	139
PRACTICE QUESTIONS	142
WHERE IN THE WORLD IS THE WEEDHEAD™	148
ACKNOWLEDGEMENTS & CREDITS	151

The WeedHead™ & Company; "All the Way Up" at 2018 Women Grow Leadership Summit; (L-R Back) Ice Dawson, Vida Dawson, Dasheeda Dawson, Imani Dawson; (Front) Aunt Latifah Shah

FOREWORD BY
Roz McCarthy, Founder & CEO Minorities for Medical Marijuana

We are witnessing the birth of America's next big business sector. Legal cannabis, still in its infancy, is already the country's fastest growing industry. In 2018, the US legal marijuana market generated 10.4 billion dollars, and is growing at an impressive 24 percent annually. At the time of this writing, eleven states and Washington DC have legalized cannabis for adult use. Medical marijuana is currently legal in 33 states.

Right now, the cannabis industry is growing from the ground up. As the CEO and founder of Minorities for Medical Marijuana (M4MM), a non-profit organization committed to cultivating a culturally inclusive cannabis industry that values, respects and celebrates diversity of thought, experience and opportunities, I've spoken to literally thousands of people who are eager to learn more about the industry and join the approximately 200,000 Americans currently working with what was once considered a national scourge.

My goal has always been to open the doors of the industry as wide as possible, and make it inclusive, equitable and beneficial for all, particularly those from communities marginalized by cannabis prohibition and its unequal enforcement. Legalization isn't simply an economic issue, it's also about justice and helping those thrown in jail and those whose lives were ruined and neighborhoods destroyed because America used its draconian drug laws to repress communities of color. Now that legal cannabis is the country's fastest growing sector, the same people who were harassed, jailed and marginalized for marijuana possession have been largely locked out of the economic boom. Wealth is a huge barrier to entry, but education has become the great equalizer, granting smart, enterprising individuals the ability to join the industry, even without access to capital.

Minorities for Medical Marijuana 2018 Leadership Retreat, Atlanta GA

There are plenty of instructors and newly crowned experts promising cannabis education, but few can deliver like Dasheeda Dawson, a trailblazer, respected industry thought-leader and seasoned executive whose commitment to rebranding the plant, removing the stigma of prohibition and restoring communities devastated by America's war on drugs has made her a powerful advocate. I'm grateful to have her expertise on M4MM's executive team as Chief Strategy Officer and believe everyone curious about cannabis should have an advisor like Dasheeda.

The WeedHead™ & Company presents Bud & Bougie Denver 2018 featuring The Dank Duchess

A Princeton and Rutgers grad, Dasheeda is passionate about education and its potential to broaden and equalize the cannabis industry. She's shared her strategic approach to the green rush at conferences, panel discussions and among her personal and professional networks. Dasheeda has helped countless individuals successfully enter this blossoming industry, and to hit the ground running, avoiding many of the pitfalls and too-good-to-be-true gimmicks that befall those who fail to adequately prepare. This workbook is a synthesis of the information she's compiled as an industry leader, combined with exercises designed to help readers create a strategic plan for successfully entering the space as an employee, investor or entrepreneur.

The WeedHead™ & Company in partnership with the Beverly Gray Business Exchange Center; Buffalo, NY

www.theweedhead.com

She used her brilliant mind, that pre-cannabis ran some of the world's largest and most successful consumer brands, to construct a pathway into the sector that leverages a person's skills and strengths. This book delves deep into the industry, beyond the plant touching positions to all aspects of the business, including ancillary roles that in many cases require little more than a good idea, genuine effort and enough resilience to stay the course.

Dasheeda has mastered the get-rich-smartly approach, and shares her insights with both candor and compassion. With this book, her students receive foundational knowledge and the confidence to bring their existing talents into the brave new world of cannabis. Her method of focusing on the less sexy but more stable parts of the cannabis industry helps foster overall growth and offers everyone the opportunity to benefit from the burgeoning sector, regardless of their starting position.

Whether the goal is simply getting a good job, or creating generational wealth, 'How to Succeed in the Cannabis Industry' shows the way. All you have to do is bring the will.

INTRODUCTION
How to Use This Workbook

When I first set out to write a book chronicling my experiences crossing over into the legal cannabis industry, my initial goal was to provide hacks for ambitious entrepreneurs and professionals like me to better navigate the burgeoning industry. However, when the game changes on a dime, as it often does in legal cannabis, it demands new rules to keep successfully moving forward. Now in its third edition, *How to Succeed in the Cannabis Industry* is an interactive and inspirational educational guide for anyone from virtually any background interested in the legal market. Opportunities abound, ranging from health benefits to social impact to business ventures. This is an exciting time to join the hemp and marjiuana movement. Yet, after meeting so many individuals across the global legal markets, it is clear that a common misconception persists among newbies and those aspiring to be in cannabis: *breaking into the industry is the same as hitting a "gold mine" with immediate returns.*

This false impression has prevented the cannabis industry from realizing its true potential. Now on the fourth or fifth wave of new entrants to the market since California introduced medical marijuana back in 1996, we still have a lot of work to do to legitimize, stabilize and diversify the industry. With this mission at the forefront of my mind, I wrote this book to help those individuals who are really passionate about finding success in the cannabis industry and willing to put in work. As the first in The WeedHead™ workbook series, this book provides the foundation of cannabis re-education and industry insights, intended to inspire advocates, entrepreneurs and consumers towards innovative problem solving and disruptive solutions that will benefit the global industry and society at-large.

If your life is anything like mine, between work, family and the ever evolving business landscape, there are times when it feels like there just aren't enough hours in the day. As a mother and CEO, I'm increasingly picky about the books I read. I suspect you might be particular about what you read as well. At the same time, I know firsthand that it can often take just one pivotal idea for a book or resource to change a life or mindset forever. I believe this workbook is one of those resources truly worth the investment of your time and effort.

"In fact, this book is truly designed to adjust your mindset..."

Legalization has literally created a $10 billion industry almost overnight and industry experts, myself included, believe the cannabis plant, which includes both marijuana and hemp, could ring up another $500 billion worth of market applications over the next ten years. Cannabis legalization has a global financial impact, with multiple countries moving towards decriminalization and/or legalization in the last two years. In addition to this unprecedented financial impact that legalization creates, there are also many health and social justice aspects that are just as important. By the time you're finished reading and completing the self-assessment questions contained in this workbook, **you** will understand how you can fit in and take advantage of this new industry. But, before we get started, because I want you to get the most out of this workbook, let me quickly explain how to best use this guide.

This workbook is designed and organized to be interactive. It starts off appraising your skills and abilities, as these will be the foundation for your success in the industry. Although this initial assessment occurs at the beginning, it's important for you to continue to evaluate, innovate and refine your thinking as you navigate the rest of the book and learn more about the industry. Leveraging market insights and real science concepts, this workbook will point you in the right direction as you start your journey to cross over into the cannabis industry regardless of your skillset. In fact, this book is truly designed to adjust your mindset as it pertains to the cannabis plant, updating your knowledge and debunking myths ingrained for generations. Being open to this necessary and ongoing re-education will offer you the best chance at success as you enter the industry.

To educate and inspire, I have provided specific brand examples throughout the book highlighting pioneering companies and individuals that are leading the way in various sectors of the industry. Google and social media search will be an important companion as you start to dig further into the specific brands and topics discussed. As I often say during my webinars and courses, the cannabis industry is a massive iceberg and this first workbook only covers the tip. With that in mind, I have strategically identified, synthesized and outlined the most important introductory topics based on my experience as a cannabis patient, global legalization advocate and successful business strategist. The industry is vast but, I have touched on everything at a high level within this book to ensure that any and everyone can understand how to best transition into the legal market.

"Think BIG, Start Small, Act Fast"

I encourage you to walk through and **work through** the book multiple times. There is no one designated path to success and you may find that as you increase your knowledge, answers about your own role may start to transform into more elaborate plans with important partners and stakeholders. Perhaps you have already started in the industry but are finding that path more difficult than expected. This workbook can help passionate and committed individuals to carve out many viable pathways to pivot strategically. We are all wearing many hats as entrepreneurs in the cannabis space, but it is clear those that choose to wear the hats that fit them best and that fit together best are finding success faster because of synergistic effects. Be prepared to test your ideas, to learn quickly and to make changes based on your insights.

Success in the cannabis industry requires everyone to think big, start small and act fast. However, the most important part is to start. My team and I are committed to helping you understand the legal cannabis industry and to give you everything you need to succeed in the **Green Rush.**

So, without further delay, let's get started!

Dasheeda Dawson AKA The WeedHead™ at Bud & Bougie Denver 2018

The purpose of this workbook is to teach you how to leverage and invest your most valuable assets into the legal cannabis industry. Those valuable assets include your skills, capabilities, passions, time and money.

One of the best things about the emerging cannabis industry is that the industry is just starting to experience formal development and legitimacy. This is literally the beginning of a global, multi-billion dollar industry, and there is room for everyone regardless of skill set or experience. No matter your passion, you can deploy it here and build a side hustle, or an empire, depending on your goals.

> **"There is room for everyone regardless of skill set or experience."**

This workbook takes entrepreneurs and professionals step by step through the often complicated, yet oversimplified, cannabis industry, highlighting the biggest white space opportunities across the different sectors and emerging roles to help you find your place in this space.

I'll begin by sharing my own story and how I became involved in the legal cannabis industry, but before we jump into me, let's identify the WHO, WHAT, and WHY about you first! If you do nothing else in this workbook, authentically answering these first three questions will be the single most important driver of your success in this industry.

1. Who are you? Include any details you would want to include in your cannabis crossover story.

2. What are your current skills and abilities? Based on you currently know, how might they be applied in the cannabis space? Include anything for which you have experience and/or credentials. As you learn more about the industry, you should come back to this question to refine your answers.

HINT: Skills are usually things for which you have received training. Abilities are usually things considered innate or "born this way".

3. Why do you want to cross over into the cannabis industry? How might your skills and abilities be applied to the space?

TARGET TO THC:
Crossing Over Into Cannabis

I was climbing the corporate ladder, and doing everything one would typically do to ensure a successful corporate career. Then, I suffered a catastrophic blow. My mom passed away unexpectedly. Grief led me to question everything about my life, and ultimately walk away from my flourishing professional career to move west to Arizona, a legal medical marijuana state. Like so many people that I've encountered, becoming a cannabis patient *first* was transformative for me, particularly as a Black woman.

So many of us have grown up under siege. I'm from East New York, a tough Brooklyn, NY neighborhood. It's not the 'new' Brooklyn that has become world renowned for artists, hipsters and craft beer. It was, and remains, hardcore. I grew up during the height of America's war on drugs. I swore off all illegal substances as a child, including marijuana or cannabis. Instead, with the support of my family, I followed a very straight and narrow path: studying hard, excelling at sports, going to prep school, and then to Princeton University. I was a basketball player, so I approached life in a very strategic and disciplined way. I stayed as far away from illicit activity as I could.

Against this very Spartan existence, my mom consumed cannabis all my life. She and her friends smoked regularly. However, for me, there was a complete disconnect from their behavior and the bleak picture of drug addicts, degenerates denounced by Nancy Reagan and the "Just Say No" campaign. My sisters and I always knew that mom was a cannabis user. We just never talked about it within my family. Internally, it just never seemed like a big deal or a cardinal sin (unless you got caught). I guess in the back of our minds, we realized that bad people weren't the only ones consuming, even if we couldn't articulate it.

Fast forward a few decades. After graduating from Princeton and nearly finishing medical school, I decided that business was my calling. I received my MBA from Rutgers Business School and eventually landed in Minneapolis working as a Target Corporation senior executive. Around the same time, my mother was diagnosed with breast cancer. She moved in with me to seek treatment at the Mayo Clinic, renowned for its world class medical facilities. Despite the amazing care she received, my mother suffered through chemo and needed cannabis for comfort. She couldn't eat, she couldn't sleep, she wasn't herself, and more than anything else; she was anxious about dying. Mom had chronic ailments on top of the cancer that left her in unbearable pain, battling inflammation, and intestinal issues. Chemo aggravated all of these issues and despite countless prescribed drugs, often within tough side effects, only cannabis actually helped her pain, reduced her anxiety and improved her appetite. and inflamed them. Many times, she experienced relief within one or two puffs of her joint!

Meanwhile, the icy cold Minnesota winter triggered my own chronic inflammation. Years of playing basketball caught up with me, leaving me with arthritis in multiple joints. I'd wake up feeling like a tin woman, needing time just to get moving. I was under the age of 35, but felt about eighty years old inside. After watching me struggle with pain and stiffness, one day Mom invited me to smoke with her. I resisted, but she persisted, saying "Oh child, come smoke a joint with your Mama" in a – you only live once kind of way. So I sat down and consumed cannabis for the first time with my mother. Though this was not my first time smoking marijuana, it was in fact my first time smoking with wellness intent. The next day, I felt so much better!

At first, I didn't know what to make of it. Even with a molecular biology degree and medical school education, I couldn't understand how cannabis, a schedule I drug, could be at all beneficial. I marveled at the impact of my first "conscious" consumption. All of my body's joints felt less painful and less inflamed. I'm also typically an insomniac, because my brain is always on. Unless I force myself to sleep, I can stay up all night, which of course served me well through Princeton and b-school. However, I wasn't getting any younger and it was beginning to take a toll on my functionality and personality. With night time usage, I actually slept through the night.

I quickly learned that this plant actually has countless therapeutic medicinal properties that are not yet fully understood. And more importantly, I began to learn the nuances of my endocannabinoid system. But, getting my cannabis came at a cost. First and foremost, buying from an illegal and unregulated market for me meant a different product every time. And, often times, I didn't really know what I was getting when I got it.

I started to quietly experiment on myself, and realized almost immediately that cannabis doesn't change my ability to be highly functional and productive. I would argue that getting a good night's rest and reducing my chronic pain actually enhanced my capabilities. Seems logical, but yet I was still so secretive about my usage to avoid judgement from my peers. But, let's be real, I didn't want to lose my job! I still went to work every day and I quickly became a top performer. In real life, I literally became the Olivia Pope of Target Corporation, with the ability to tackle and turn around failing business units. **Real talk:** I came to work with less anxiety, and probably less stress than most managers, most likely because I was utilizing cannabis.

But, I would not have chosen to leave my job, or the comfortable life I had built, to come out of the cannabis closet. So I understand why so many are hesitant to express interest in this new industry. It took a life changing event for that to happen. After moving back to New York to lead teams at Victoria's Secret and another major Fortune 500 Company, my life was upended.

My mom was seemingly in remission, and then out of nowhere she passed away. Mom literally went to the doctor for a routine check up on a Monday, and by Friday she was gone. It was the type of tragedy that happened so fast that it shakes a person to the core. I felt like I had to disappear. I took three weeks off from work. The first day when I returned, I realized I had to resign. It was time for me to go because, I felt an urgency of purpose. My mom was gone, and I never knew my father, so I felt like an orphan. After helping to pay for my mother's funeral expenses and settling her estate, I knew I had to do more than just climb the corporate ladder, as a slave to someone else's bottom line. My sisters and I had always had successful side hustle businesses. But, in my gut, I knew that would not be enough to generate the wealth required to last for generations; for my tribe, my son and for his children.

Looking back at my career at Target Corporation, I helped the company earn what I would conservatively estimate as a half billion dollars in incremental revenue, through my analysis, strategies and execution management. But, I really hadn't even seen a fraction of 1% of that. I abandoned the corporate life, at first to heal and cope with my grief. I moved to Arizona and with the help of my mom's sister, Aunt Latifah, entered the medical marijuana community through the patient side. She was already a medical marijuana patient and guided me through the process.

Immediately, I reaped more benefits from a legalized market than I could imagine. I was suffering from undiagnosed anxiety and PTSD as a result of growing up in East New York and chronic inflammation throughout my body, with unknown autoimmune issues that behave like lupus, though I have yet to be formally diagnosed. Issues that I'm sure a lot of other people have to deal with as well, particularly Black women and other people of color. The legal medical marijuana market consistently offered me options, time for openly learning, and more consumer protection as compared to my prior experience.

That said, my experience entering the industry as a patient was still challenging starting from the process of obtaining my medical marijuana card. The long wait times to see a medical professional and unclear payment processes could have easily deterred the average person. Then, once I walked into my first dispensary, while I was pleased to freely ask questions and select different strains, I had an extremely poor consumer experience as a patient with real ailments and as a shopper with real questions about "brands". If I compared my experience to the illegal market, it was certainly an improvement. However, it was a far cry from mainstream retail consumer experiences.

"You can be highly functional and utilize cannabis all day long."

As a consumer marketing expert, I felt compelled to help. I knew my skills could help to re-educate, to rebrand the industry and to remove the stigma associated with being a patient. You can most certainly be highly functional and utilize cannabis all day long. Once I entered the industry, and began traveling to legal states like Colorado, California, Oregon and Washington, too often, I was the only Black person in the boardroom. I knew I needed to share my story with other people of color. There are young brothers and sisters back home in Brooklyn, NY that are still being targeted and arrested for marijuana possession despite a decriminalization law on the books for over forty years, which disturbs me. It became clear to me that as the industry evolves, we need to be more present as entrepreneurs and investors. As the saying goes, "If you don't have a seat at the table, you're probably on the menu."

I've now been in the business for nearly four years. I began my journey as the founder and CEO of MJM Strategy, the cannabis industry's first minority-led, digital-focused strategy and management consulting firm. We have worked on all types of projects in the industry from cultivation SOPs to strategic brand marketing to supply chain operations to finance, depending on the client's needs.

Today, I am focused on The WeedHead™ & Company, an education and lifestyle brand for conscious consumers and professionals curious about legitimately participating in the legal cannabis industry.

This book is for anyone interested in the growing cannabis industry, from entrepreneurs thinking about entering the field, to private investors. In fact, all professions are welcome: contractors, doctors, lawyers, nurses, consultants, advisors. It will take a group effort to help build this new industry.

This is not a "get rich quick scheme" but rather I will cover the basics to help you identify opportunities best suited for you and your goals. We will dive into the different sectors of the cannabis industry, as well as strategies for breaking in as an employee or an entrepreneur. Once you've finished this book, you'll have the information you need to enter the cannabis industry and succeed.

Welcome to the cannabis community!

PART 1:
Roles in the Legal Cannabis Industry

In this section, we will dig deeper into roles within the legal cannabis industry. Like any other industry, the legal cannabis business is comprised of specific segments with distinct roles, such as growers, distributors, resellers, dispensaries and retailers. These roles ensure that the industry thrives and becomes future-proof. So, if you're interested in the business, the first question that you must ask yourself is "what are the most critical and fastest growing positions in the industry, and what role could I possibly play?"

4. Part 1 Teaser Quiz: Name 10 roles you believe are important within the legal cannabis industry.

CULTIVATOR/ FARMER:
Start Growing Your Own Cannabis

As cannabis is a plant, the first and most obvious roles in this developing industry is as a cultivator, grower or farmer, depending on the size of your operation. This is what we call a "plant-touching" position that you can do as an entrepreneur or as an employee/contractor for a company. This is one of the industry's most important functions because growers cultivate the cannabis plants used for further downstream processing and manufacturing. As you might already guess, this is also the most common role that comes to mind when referencing the industry, largely due to a simplistic perspective, built from experiences in illegal markets. It may also seem as if this is the role with the largest return on investment or ROI. However, from my experience in the industry to date, that is often not the case. To legally start a cannabis cultivation business in most states, the costs are astronomical, requiring significant start up capital for land/property, equipment, lights, licensing fees and consultants. Land and property that is zoned for cultivation also presents a challenge for most individuals. Yet, even if you have the skill, capital and property, you must obtain a license to grow (and sell) commercially.

As legalization grows in popularity, we have already seen a limited number of licenses made available in most states, at least initially. Many people within the industry compare obtaining a license to winning a lottery ticket! Once obtained, being a licensed plant-touching entrepreneur is without question the riskiest role in our current political and economic climate. Therefore, I highly recommend that you start out with one of the other potential roles outlined in this workbook. For those still determined to touch the plant legally, here are a few "cheat codes" to help you play that game better:

- ☑ Start with hemp! It is easier legally with often more lenient licensing requirements with much lower fees. For more insights about the hemp side of the market, you can find more information on page 82 of this workbook.
- ☑ Move to a state with better policies and/or less competition. Or you can partner with relatives or friends in states with less competition. Examples include Oklahoma or Missouri.
- ☑ Be a cultivation consultant to a larger company. Let them do the work of securing a license and remaining legally compliant. You just focus on cultivation.
- ☑ Be a reputable brand with great flower or distinguished cultivation techniques. This is the hardest because this is highly subjective and widely claimed by most master cultivators. However, local cultivators can develop brand equity with consistent delivery of great results under a brand name. The next step is negotiating a consulting and/or royalty deal with a larger company to capitalize on the brand name.

5. Why would entering the cannabis industry as a plant-touching entrepreneur or grower be the riskiest proposition? List 3 or more reasons.

6. If planning to cultivate/grow/farm, what other roles will be important to have on your team and license application regardless of state.

A) *Legal:*

B) *Marketing & Sales:*

C) *Finance (Planning & Management):*

7. Using your current skills, how can you enter the cannabis industry without handling the actual plant?

PARALLELS IN HISTORY:
California Gold Rush

Success in the cannabis industry, which many like to call the "Green Rush" can actually be found by first analyzing comparable points in history, where new industries were being developed. Many people reference the end of alcohol prohibition as a comparable experience because we are moving an illegal and unregulated substance into a highly regulated, revenue-driving industry. While I agree this is an important historical reference as we consider the possibilities of types of regulations, I believe as we learn more about the science of the plant and its true goodness, we will become less tied to the alcohol comparison.

Another comparison in history that really provided me the most insight on how to succeed in cannabis, has been the California Gold Rush. If you don't recall learning about this in your high school history class, take a minute to do a quick Google search. For the sake of giving you the tools to get started, here are a few of the noteworthy highlights. During the 1840s and 50s, people from all over the United States and even abroad flooded into California, hoping to strike it rich in search of the precious metal, gold. As you can imagine, extracting gold from mines is an extremely difficult and arduous process requiring back-breaking labor. Many gold miners risked their lives and fortunes attempting to gain wealth this way. However, very few gold miners actually made money during the Gold Rush. Most were lucky if they recouped their expenses.

8. **Outside of panning for gold, what other ways might someone have been able to profit from California's Gold Rush? List three or more.**

9. **As you conduct your initial Google search, what can you learn from the Gold Rush example as you consider entering the new Green Rush? What are potential pitfalls to avoid? List two or more.**

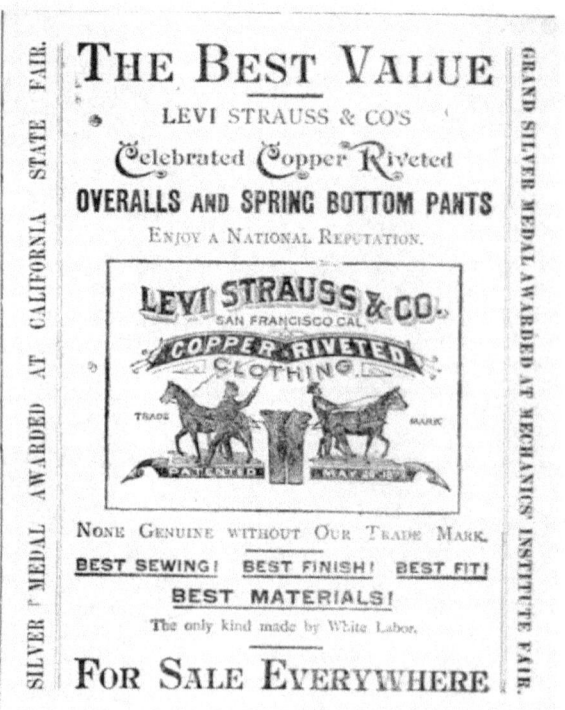 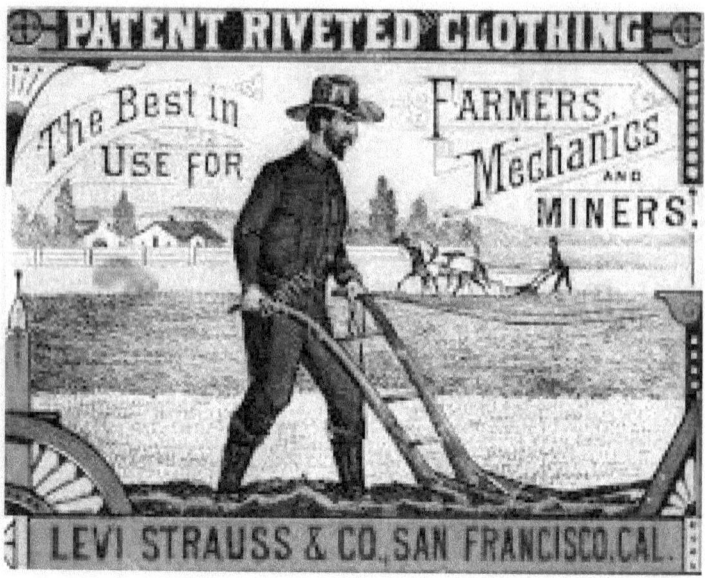

Similar to the legal cannabis industry, many people faced discrimination and were unable to participate directly as miners. They didn't have enough funding or business resources to get in the traditional way. These unique circumstances proved to be a very lucky perspective for those still determined to capitalize on the Gold Rush. For example, a German immigrant living in New York traveled to California and saw a different opportunity to strike it rich during the Gold Rush. Instead of searching for gold, he decided to sell basic goods to the gold miners. This was, for him, a much safer way to make a profit. Due to circumstances, this entrepreneur had to be more clever. He soon realized that his miner friends needed equipment and goods to search for gold they hoped would make them rich.

Eventually, the immigrant's most profitable product became a new style of durable pants that withstood the extreme conditions facing the gold miners. This is now known as a classic "Picks and Shovels" methodology and that German immigrant was none other than blue jeans pioneer, Levi Strauss. His rugged pants were such a success, that they remain one of the world's most common articles of clothing.

We are in the midst of another transformational industry rush, but this time, it's the **Green Rush** into the legal cannabis market.

10. Now that you have learned about the story of Levi Strauss and the Gold Rush, can you list and describe 3 additional "Picks and Shovels" profit opportunities that probably existed during the Gold Rush?

Opportunity 1

Opportunity 2

Opportunity 3

OPPORTUNITIES IN CANNABIS:
The Picks & Shovels Mindset

The most exciting (and profitable) companies in the cannabis industry, will be those that provide services and goods to the plant-touching cannabis operations. These companies are currently making millions and will continue to make more money, the same way innovative and solution-focused businesses did during the Gold Rush. This is because cannabis operations need materials like soil, lights, growing and hydroponic equipment, ventilation systems and services like packaging, quality control, security and transportation.

With the "Picks and Shovels" mindset, companies can avoid the risks growers and producers face such as bad crops, legal regulations and pricing. In fact, there is another unreported reason why the legal marijuana market is going to grow much bigger and faster than anyone predicts: Illegal marijuana operations are also feeding the legal marijuana market!

"Success is about seeing *opportunity* where others don't."

Check the statistics. In 2017, California's legal marijuana market was valued at nearly $3 billion. But, it grew over $23 billion worth of marijuana. The remaining $20 billion came from the legacy markets: the illegal growing, selling and usage of cannabis. Although it is an unorthodox notion to consider, even illegal cannabis growers still need to buy soil, lighting, ventilation systems and such, which gives ancillary services and products access to more customers driving extra billions in the overall cannabis market. These numbers have increased as a result of California's status as an adult-use market, effective January 1, 2018. In 2018, California's status changed to an adult-use market. Due to significant changes to regulations and widespread retail contraction, legal marijuana sales slid to $2.5 billion in 2018, yet other areas of the industry continued to grow. However, despite overall sales reduction, California's first year of legal adult-use is by far still the largest legal market in the nation, eclipsing Colorado by nearly 60% more sales.

11. Can you provide 3 other ancillary products or services that cannabis growers (legal or illegal) would need to purchase to run their businesses successfully?

Ancillary "Picks and Shovels" Opportunity #1

Ancillary "Picks and Shovels" Opportunity #2

Ancillary "Picks and Shovels" Opportunity #3

Individuals can profit from the "Picks and Shovels" strategy in the cannabis industry by being consultants and applying existing skills to the bold new marketplace. For example, when marijuana becomes legal in a state, naturally, more people find themselves with the freedom and the desire to grow the plant, but with limited information and resources. So, they turn to the experts. As a result, cultivation classes are taught and reference books purchased. Growing rooms are built with complete infrastructure including electricity, adequate water supply and professional space planning. This means contractors, builders, electricians and plumbers have found a new niche where they can use their skills to build growing rooms. There are now even specialized greenhouse and grow room builders in the market.

This is also a good way to enter the market if you have a complementary skill set. It also allows you to test your abilities and experience against the market, and establish a permanent foothold in a growing industry.

In the next section, industry opportunities and areas of growth will be explored in greater detail. You'll be able to see exactly where the jobs and white space markets are, and how you can be competitive.

12. List and describe 3 skills that you currently have and how that might be applied using a "Picks and Shovels" mindset in the cannabis industry.

Skill Set & Application #1

Skill Set & Application #2

Skill Set & Application #3

TOP ROLES IN CANNABIS:

Grow Room Construction
Greenhouse Construction
Security Design & Installation
Interior Design
IT/SEO
Software Development
Social Marketing
Event Planner
Electrical
Product Development
Manufacturing
Plumbing
Carpentry
Professional Services

If you want to follow the "Picks and Shovels" mindset for success in the cannabis industry, there are a variety of sectors in which to place yourself and your suitable skills and talents. As you can see from the above examples, opportunities abound across disciplines. From carpentry to social media marketing, the skills needed to fully develop this industry are immense. Whatever you do, you can find a place in this growing industry.

One of the earliest examples of this strategy involves a key executive of trailblazing dispensary Harborside Health Center, which gained fame after being featured on Discovery Channel's "Weed Wars" in 2011. Yoli Felix, the dispensary's creative director, is an interior designer by trade. She had no previous background in cannabis, but she used her years of experience to design beautiful dispensary spaces for the Harborside brand. Her story is a perfect example of how someone can take their skills and expertise from a mainstream industry and crossover successfully in the cannabis industry.

During my time as a leading consultant in the industry, I have encountered countless other stories like this, especially as the industry becomes increasingly popular.

Attorneys, for example, can also establish lucrative niches in cannabis. Some of the industry's biggest success stories come from attorneys who started working with cannabis clients and then leveraged their newly acquired knowledge to specialize in the cannabis industry, in some cases being pulled in to launch the cannabis practice area for large corporate law firms.

13. Pick out 3 of the roles listed above and describe how they might be applicable in a "Picks and Shovels" strategy for the cannabis industry.

Role & Application #1

Role & Application #2

Role & Application #3

PART 1:
Key Takeaways

There is a lot of excitement about the cannabis industry right now. But exactly how do you open that door? How do you turn the cannabis growth opportunity into cash in-hand? Here are key takeaways that will help you get started.

Educate yourself first. Read! Attend events. Join associations or work for an existing cannabis company. One of the mistakes many people make when trying to come into the cannabis space is not spending enough time getting educated about the industry itself. This is probably from the fear of missing out (FOMO). Cannabis is touted as the next big thing and many are rushing to carve out a place, but wind up shooting in the dark. Entrepreneurs should have a working knowledge of the industry and a solid business plan before jumping in. It's not going anywhere, and eager entrants won't lose out by taking the time to familiarize themselves with the plant, players, products, and processes behind the burgeoning sector, so that they find their place with minimal obstacles.

Learn as much as you can about cannabis and the industry. A few of my favorite books to add to your library and education: *The Pot Book* edited by Dr. Julie Holland, *ABCs of*

CBD by Shira Adler, *Vitamin Weed* by Dr. Michele Ross, and *Start Your Own Cannabis Business* by Javier Hasse.

There are also multiple cannabis conferences and expos held across the country with different themes and orientations. Attend as many as you can. Even smaller conferences will offer valuable information and most importantly, a rare opportunity for face-to-face connections.

I also recommend joining associations like Minorities for Medical Marijuana and your local state or networking organizations, such as NORML, Women Grow, or Cannagather, because these are great places to have direct contact with other budding entrepreneurs in the industry. The people on the ground will be your most valuable source of real time knowledge and insight about the industry, which is still very confined to local state markets. You get to ask them real questions and get real answers from real people.

Last but not least, consider working or volunteering for an established company or advocacy organization. There is no better way than learning on the job, and many start-ups and emerging businesses will welcome the assistance.

Customize to the industry. Cannabis is different! Standard techniques often don't work. Take sufficient time to understand what's unique. Identify and fill the special needs of the cannabis industry. Anyone looking to enter the cannabis industry must be aware that this is unlike other fields. Standard rules don't apply. Because it isn't as established as say, banking or hospitality, it's critical that prospective entrepreneurs and employees be proactive and focused on solutions. They must take the time to examine their unique skill sets and figure out how to adapt them to the industry.

The key here is looking at problems facing the industry and providing the solutions for them. This is an often overlooked classic business principle. Before you dive into cannabis you need to ask yourself, 'What are the challenges? What are the problems they have that I can solve?' and 'How do I find a unique place within this industry so that I can really carve out something special for myself?'

14. Now that you have ideas about your potential "picks and shovels" opportunities, list your top three, along with ways each will resolve a current problem for the cannabis industry.

Idea #1

> *PROBLEM:*
>
>
> *POTENTIAL SOLUTION:*

Idea #2

> *PROBLEM:*
>
>
> *POTENTIAL SOLUTION:*

Idea #3

> *PROBLEM:*
>
>
> *POTENTIAL SOLUTION:*

15. What special skills or know-how can you use with your "picks and shovels" idea to gain entry into the industry?

16. What can you do to make your offering unique?

17. What are some of the needs that you can satisfy in the cannabis space with your offering?

18. How can you become an advocate for the cannabis industry in your area of expertise?

19. What are the key industry-related organizations in your state, region or area that you can volunteer for, to gain experience?

20. List some local start up organizations that you can reach out to, for assisting with daily tasks, shadowing opportunities and possibly offering your services pro bono or at a discounted rate.

PART 2:
Sectors in the Cannabis Industry

In Part 2, I'm going to cover the various sectors in the cannabis industry and the emerging areas most in demand. Here, we'll take a look at specific niches, study examples of successful companies within those sectors, and review the areas with the greatest opportunities. As we are only really scratching the surface on information, I highly recommend using Google and LinkedIn to do a deeper dive into any companies or brands of interest noted as successful examples.

GENETICS:
Seeds
Clones
Tissues

While I feel strongly that people should focus on ancillary businesses that don't directly involve touching the plant, any discussion of the industry must begin with cannabis itself. Plants are at the very core of this industry. Genetics play a vital role. Cannabis plant cultivation generally involves seeds and clones cut from mother plants. Right now, tissue culture is a popular method of cultivation, as it allows producers to manufacture more clones at a lower price in a shorter period of time. This is important due to the chemical complexity of the plant.

There are a variety of different strains and each strain has unique cannabinoid and terpene profiles. This means that a deep understanding and knowledge of genetics are skills in demand offering huge dividends for those with the requisite capabilities. For example, Mimosa by Symbiotic Genetics is a rising star in the cannabis community. This strain has been praised for its outstanding fruity, citrus rind aroma and pleasurable mid level buzz. Mimosa is a genetic cross of two strains, Clementine and Purple Punch. It is known to contain respectable percentages of the terpenes, limonene and beta-caryophyllene with its percentage of THC ranging anywhere from 17 to 28. More recently, their strain placed 4th in "Best Outdoor Flower" at the 2018 Emerald Cup. Easily, the Emerald

Cup is known as the largest, most respected organic outdoor cannabis competition in the world. This, along with other "cups" or competitions, is how new growers can introduce and prove themselves to a global community of cannabis connoisseurs.

Seeds

In Europe, seed companies are the biggest players in the industry because the production and marketing of seeds is legal. There are virtually no major dispensaries on the continent, so most cannabis is grown and sold by individuals or small scale establishments.

Founded in 1985, Sensi Seeds is still one of the most successful cannabis-related companies in the world. It is a Dutch company based in Amsterdam that markets cannabis seeds and other cannabis-related merchandise. It is the oldest and largest hemp seed producer with the world's largest hemp seed bank. Which brings me to a very important point. Yes, hemp is cannabis too! Most people don't realize that hemp and marijuana are in fact related scientifically. In 2018, the US Farm Bill federally legalized hemp for all 50 states. Therefore, as we speak to genetics, cultivation, and extraction, it is very important to recognize that there is significant knowledge overlap for hemp and marijuana in these areas, presenting new entrants the opportunity to capitalize on the "Green Rush" via a less risky hemp licensing pathway.

Clones

When it comes to clones, the biggest success story is Oakland California's Dark Heart Nursery. When cannabis clones were first marketed, they were very fragile specimens that stood only 1.5 to 4 inches tall. Nowadays, clones produced by this company are strong and vigorous specimens that regularly stand close to a foot tall! Many of California's large scale cannabis operations have been started from Dark Heart's clones. Certainly, a good number of cultivators globally prefer to develop their own clones from seeds to ensure they can market themselves as "seed-to-sale" growers, but launching a new grow with a solid lot of healthy clones can save a large operation on time and money as they are getting up and running. In this case, the transaction is business-to-business (B2B) and often involves transfer of thousands of clones, separated into many different strain groups.

Like a landscaper purchasing for foundation planting, growhouse general managers and lead cultivators spend countless hours strategically planning and then purchasing appropriate clones to achieve the desired harvest. In addition to ensuring they are growing the right strains, they scrutinize the size and health of clone batches by strain, looking for any signs that might prove to be a risk for the long term output of the plants. Within the United States legal market, every seed is tracked to a clone, every clone sold is also tracked to fully grown plant, and every plant is tracked to its final processing. This is all done via state-required software. Therefore, individuals that are interested in focusing on clones should be prepared to provide and validate fairly detailed genetic information about the clones in addition to growing conditions and regimen. Imagine handing over a 6 week old puppy to new owners. To ensure the best transition, the new puppy parents would need to know the established regimen, including perhaps any issues that may have arisen during the first few weeks of life. Imagine the puppy had to be transported for hours and subject to unknown or less than ideal conditions. All of this must be taken into consideration as you consider handling and selling clones, which are essentially baby cannabis plants. This is also why businesses in this sector are commonly referred to as nurseries.

In markets where homegrow is legal, clones are also available to be sold business-to-consumer (B2C) via retail dispensaries. This is actually fairly common in the California market, particularly with large dispensaries creating separate displays and consumer experience to market their clones available on-hand. As more states allow for homegrow, we will see this particular sector continue to grow in the business to consumer market. While the average consumer is far less discerning than a growhouse general manager, many of the same rules apply to successfully market and sell clones in a B2C model.

Tissue Cultures

Because the cultivation of plants via seeds and clones is critically important in this industry, it is essential that it be done right from the beginning. Therefore, we can't talk about genetics without also talking about plant tissue culture technologies. Tissue culturing is the process of propagating fresh plants by growing them from the cellular level in a controlled and sterile environment. Much like a genetic tabula rasa, this process, also known as micropropagation, allows master cultivators to sterilize and stabilize the plant's genetics at the cellular level.

Admittedly, as a molecular biologist, I am a total geek about this topic, particularly as it has been applied to the cannabis industry. Believe it or not, the use of tissue culturing in plants has been around for a while, apparently started by the orchid industry back in the 1950's. Through the use of this process, plant scientists can mitigate risks that insects and bacteria can pose to the plant.

In the case of orchids, the technique has been used to preserve an endangered species of the plant. Similarly, as cannabis genetics becomes more cross-bred, tissue culturing allows farmers to rejuvenate the genetic line, even eliminate or cleanse bad genetic expression that could lead to poor plant health and other genetic defects. Another important benefit of using tissue cultures is the ability to maintain a much larger library of genetic variations without having to dedicate the space and labor to maintain mother plants.

Despite challenges with prohibition, cannabis genetics have been studied for decades. There is a wealth of great genetic material and knowledge within the current cannabis community. However, with legal concerns, most of the information has stayed within an exclusive circle of the cultivation community. Today, there are more opportunities to learn more openly, especially as more universities and STEM programs begin to see the value in teaching about cannabis. At this point, entering the genetics sector of the industry takes a background in science, preferably biology and a strong understanding of genetics. Although a degree is not essential, it is becoming more and more preferred, especially for greenhouse general managers or master cultivator roles.

What's most important is a passion for cultivation, genetics and understanding the real science of the plant. For those still pursuing studies or willing to be an apprentice, I would highly recommend reaching out to thought leaders in the space, such as master cannabis geneticist Dr. Reggie Gaudino, Ph.D. As the President of California-based, Steep Hill Labs, he oversees the scientific research and development for the world's largest cannabis science and technology company. Under his leadership, the company has developed GenKit™, the first cannabis DNA-based sex testing allowing growers to identify male and CBD-rich seedlings in days without flowering!

In short, all of the advances in cannabis genetics and use of real science methodology have created financial and time advantages for businesses that have applied these insights. Therefore, if you are already an experienced farmer, agriculturist, or geneticist, you can be a valuable addition to a cannabis leadership team as a consultant or employee.

21. Have a passion for biology or life sciences? In what ways can you bring your passion and know-how to the genetics segment of the cannabis industry?

22. In reference to seeds, what can you offer to the industry? Do you have a distinct strain to bring to market? Is it rare or unique? Is there a shortage in certain markets?

23. What techniques and capabilities can you bring to the cultivation aspect? Can you offer ways to improve sustainability and reduce waste?

CULTIVATION:
Nursery
Sun Grown
Indoor
Organic

Once the genetics are selected, planting is the next step. There are multiple methods of cultivation, which yield cannabis with different properties and characteristics. Commercial cultivation usually starts in a nursery.

There are 3 main ways of growing cannabis:

1. **Outdoor Growing:** This is where plants are grown in an open field with plenty of natural sunlight and is how cannabis has been cultivated for thousands of years. People are often surprised to learn that Oregon is one of the best places for outdoor growing, with some counties experiencing 300+ days of sunshine in a year! That said, most outdoor-grown lovers are obsessed with plants grown in the Emerald Triangle, the northern region of California where Humboldt, Mendocino, and Trinity counties converge. Cannabis grown in this region can be upwards of 15 feet tall due to what people believe to be the most ideal, natural cannabis growing conditions in the world. In fact, the cannabis flower grown in this region commands a higher price point than much of the other product being cultivated and sold at commercial scale within the state.

2. **Greenhouse Growing:** Common throughout the California market, cannabis plants are grown in greenhouses where cultivators can manipulate the temperature and light cycle to get higher quality yield than growing outdoors. Many cultivators believe this is one of the best ways to grow cannabis on a large scale because it can leverage all of the benefits of outdoor and indoor growing combined without some of the drawbacks, including inclement weather or high carbon footprint.

3. **Indoor Growing:** Similar to greenhouse growing, cultivators get higher quality yields by exerting more control over the growth cycle than the outdoor method. However, indoor growing uses high-intensity lamps that require a large amount of energy, which drives an increase in the company's carbon footprint.

The WeedHead & Company in partnership with the Office of NY State Senator James Sanders, Chairman for Committee on Banks; Queens NY

Nursery

A **nursery** is an ideal place to grow cannabis. Currently, the number of cultivators and grow operations using nurseries continues to increase exponentially. Just a few years ago, growers would have to produce their own clones in small rooms, almost always with inadequate equipment and resources. Those clones required time, space and significant financial investment.

Today, the process has become more streamlined because clones and tissue cultures are more readily available. As we described in the last chapter, growers of all sizes can cultivate good, clean and healthy cannabis. Generally, nurseries will grow the plants from clones and tissue cultures. Next, they can sell these live plants wholesale to cultivation businesses looking to save time and resources while starting a new growhouse. This is an opportunity for savvy entrepreneurs to grow and sell plants business-to-business (B2B) on a larger scale. As homegrow is legalized, there is more opportunity for nurseries to sell these baby plants to consumers.

24. Is growing cannabis a realistic option for you? Are you in a legalized state? If so, what are the requirements for a cultivation license? If you grow, will you sell your product to cultivators or wholesalers?

25. If you are not in a legal state, what are some unique ways to enter this sector? How can you utilize the digital space?

Hint: Look at Hemp licensing and regulations in your state!

26. Can you provide tools to aid the growing process?

Hint: Think "Picks & Shovels" mindset.

Sun Grown

As the cannabis industry grows, so does the market for the **sungrown** pesticide free variety. There are now brands that specialize in this kind of cannabis. Brands like Swami Select created by California based guru Swami Chaitanya. Chaitanya, called the "the Swami of Pot" by *Rolling Stone* magazine, is also considered a holy man who uses cannabis as inspiration. Before legalization, his picture didn't appear on the packaging, likely to reduce the possibility of arrest and prosecution. However, first as private growers, then as purveyors of Swami Select, he and partner Nikki Lastreto have been in this business for decades promoting craft cannabis.

Marigold California is another highly respected craft cannabis brand. Renowned for its sungrown quality, Marigold is a cultivator collective dedicated to growing quality cannabis with a low carbon impact. Also prominent in the craft cannabis movement is Honeydew Farms, a company based in the highly coveted Humboldt County cultivation community. It offers cannabis cultivation consulting services to large scale operations and of course, provide dispensaries with quality sungrown strains in the California market.

Lamp Grown

Lamp-grown cannabis represents another type of popular plant production. Cannabis grown indoors with artificial lighting still dominates the market, despite the high carbon footprint. The advantage of growing cannabis indoors is undeniable. The results are consistent high quality cannabis flower. A rapidly growing trend has been the use of LED lights in the cannabis industry to help improve energy efficiency without sacrificing quality indoor cultivation.

Canada, our neighbor to the north, is now one of just two countries where cannabis is fully legal. Canadian based LiveWell Foods is one of the largest indoor-grown cannabis companies in the country, with more than 1.5 million square feet of cultivation facilities and a world-class research and innovation centre. The company's stock is publicly traded on the Canadian Securities Exchange.

Ten Four Farms is an indoor cultivation brand based in Oregon. They are a great example of thinking big, while starting small. The company's operation is set up in a large repurposed storage facility, where it lamp-grows six-to-eight strains in small batches. Each cultivar or strain is meticulously bred for looks, smell and effects in order to stand out within the crowded cannabis flower market in Oregon.

Well known in the industry for over ten years, Jungle Boys is a powerhouse LA brand known best for its meticulous cultivation standard operating procedures (SOPs). From cleverly designed grow rooms to fully automated hydroponic set-up, its has largely focused on improving cultivation efficiency and producing "fire" flower for the market. For example, their process dubbed "pheno-hunting" includes searching for seeds in a respective market, then growing and discarding those strains multiple times to only bring to market the best possible version of the flower. This has allowed the brand to stand out from the rest of the market, building a unique and strong brand equity in the legal market.

In the United States, cannabis currently can't technically be called 'organic,' because it is still considered illegal under US federal law. **Organic standards** are determined by specific requirements that must be verified by USDA, an impossibility given the designation of cannabis as a schedule I drug. Growers risk, among other challenges, fines of up to $11,000 levied by the US Department of Agriculture for improper labelling. An alternate naturally-grown certification makes sense, particularly when it comes to the health and wellness benefits of the plant.

Organic

Harborside Health Center partnered with Chris Van Hook, an organic certifier for farms to adapt the protocols, techniques and procedures for the cannabis industry and create a cannabis related certification called "Clean Green". Other associations like Americans for Safe Access and the California Growers Association also have their own versions of organic certifications. Becoming a cultivator in the legal cannabis industry means becoming licensed, one of the most difficult steps to doing business in this rapidly evolving space. In most states, licensing is a complex and expensive endeavor and should be navigated with the help of project management consultants, which can tip total costs into the million dollar range!

People with the passion and desire to grow, but not millions in disposable income should focus on learning the skills of cannabis cultivation with the goal of getting employment at an established grow operation, or look to relocate to a state where the costs of entering the market are relatively low. As of 2019, here are 10 key states I would recommend exploring for lower barriers of entry:

1. Oregon (Adult)
2. Oklahoma (Medical, Hemp)
3. Missouri (Medical)
4. Illinois (Adult, Medical, Hemp)
5. Michigan (Adult)
6. Georgia (Hemp)
7. North Carolina (Hemp)
8. New Jersey (Medical, Hemp)
9. South Carolina (Hemp)
10. Ohio (Medical, Hemp)

27. If you are looking to enter into the cultivation field, what organizations in your area can help you with the process? Is there an M4MM chapter in your area?

28. How will your plants be different from the others in this segment? Are your seeds different? Are your plants grown in a greenhouse? Are your plants grown outdoors with natural sunlight?

29. What practices can you use to have your plant stand out? Will you use organic soil? What about hydroponics?

PROCESSING & MANUFACTURING:

Extraction
Infusion
Formulation
Delivery Mechanisms

Until recently, small cultivators, together with teams of trimmers, processed cannabis right at the cultivation or grow house. From a supply chain perspective, this methodology has proven inefficient and difficult. Now, there are companies that specifically handle cannabis processing. They are responsible for weighing, trimming and packaging the harvest for further distribution. After initial harvesting and trimming, if the flower or bud, as we traditionally know it, is not the intended final consumer-facing product, further processing is required to transition flower to other consumable forms such as hash, rosin, vape oil, tincture, edibles or topicals. As a result of growth in these final delivery mechanisms, extraction is a rapidly emerging sector in the cannabis industry with tremendous growth potential.

Generally, extraction is the process of removing any plant's active ingredients, concentrating them, and converting them into a form that's usable for the consumer. So, this is a process that mainstream manufacturers use for other non-cannabis, plant-based products such as in pharmaceuticals, beauty or personal care. Also, there are many ways to extract from plants using industrial processes, each with its own pros and cons within the cannabis industry. We will review the most commonly used extraction methods in cannabis today but you should know the common goal of all cannabis extraction is to isolate and remove **trichomes**, hair-like crystalline structures coating the outside surface of cannabis flower. Trichome structure and function varies depending on the plant species. In the case of cannabis, these resin glands on the surface of the flower leaves are highly concentrated in cannabinoids and terpenes.

"Hashish is considered the original solventless cannabis extract."

Solventless extracts are those made without any chemicals as solvents. **Kief** is the simplest cannabis extract and often considered the lowest quality extract form. It is made simply from trichomes broken away from dried plant material via a filter screen and minimal agitation. In fact, many uneducated consumers are keeping a stash of kief in the bottom chamber of their 3-piece herb grinders! On its own, kief is more potent than flower, ranging from 20 to 60% THC. Quality kief is light blonde or tan in color with a strong and attractive terpene aroma.

Hashish is considered the original solventless cannabis extract. Old school processing to make high-grade hash could actually involve directly-rubbing flowers and scraping the plant's resin into a ball. Obviously, hand rubbing to extract is a very labor intensive despite great end product. Therefore, the most common method for making old school hash is via a process called dry sifting. **Dry sift hash** involves rubbing dried cannabis flower over a filter screen to separate the highly concentrated trichomes into piles of kief, which is then heated and pressed into hash. While technically water is a solvent, **ice hash** is another old school cannabis extract classified as solventless in the market largely because water is generally regarded as safe. Involving only ice and water, this process has been used for thousands of years. The ice cold mixture is agitated to separate the trichomes from the leaves and strained to collect very potent concentrations of hash. Learning these age-old methods isn't as simple as taking a course in college or watching a how-to video. Ultimately, hashmakers are extraction *artists* and techniques are learned and mastered under apprenticeships. For example, The Dank Duchess is one of the only African-American hashmakers in the world. Internationally known for her delicious hash, she was the co-valedictorian of her class at Oaksterdam University and received her extraction education from direct hands-on experience with legendary hashish artist, Frenchy Cannoli. Featured on Viceland's *Bong Appetit,* she is a highly sought-after cannabis consultant and hash critic known for her impeccable techniques, ranging from cultivation to extraction. As a pioneer in the industry, she is changing the narrative and common stereotypes around concentrated cannabis consumption.

Templeballs and a hash rod flatten under their own weight as they cool. Image courtesy of The Dank Duchess

Also considered solventless, **rosin** (not to be confused with resin) is made using heat and pressure to squeeze out highly potent cannabis oil from dried and cured flowers of the plant. Unlike industrial forms of extraction, this process can be safely done in the home using something as simple as wax baking paper to surround the bud and a consumer-grade flatiron as the "rosin press". In fact, some dispensaries are now selling large scale rosin press machines with temperature controlled settings. Last year, Wal-Mart.com began selling one and quickly sold out in 24 hours! The popularity of solventless extracts like rosin continues to rapidly increase with new entrants and innovations in the market, all with the goal of creating natural and mild cannabis extract consumables.

One of the most popular methods of extraction used in cannabis today is also the least safe for consumers if not done properly. It involves using butane, hexane or other types of heavy industrial hydrocarbons as solvents. **Butane Hash Oil (BHO)** became very popular in the early 2000's and still remains a staple in most legal market dispensaries. It is extremely popular among homemade extraction artists. However, butane is highly flammable and should not be handled outside of certified industrial labs during processing. Improper handling in the past has caused many infamous explosions within apartment buildings and homes. More recently, because of concerns about carcinogens and unknown side effects from consumption, usage of these heavy solvents has slowed considerably and are actively being monitored in the industry. As states begin to monitor and test solvent levels, there is industry confusion regarding the terms "Solvent-FREE" vs. "SolventLESS". Fundamentally, if a solvent is used in the extraction is can never be considered solventless, but with excellent purge technique, products can be cleaned to the solvent-free level. Solvent-based extracts like BHO can be tested and certified as "solvent-free" through purging and cleaning to remove solvent residue to below required limits for safe human consumption. Removing solvent residue is a technical process that should also be conducted in a lab for the safety of manufacturers and consumers.

Along the same line of creating safer and cleaner extraction-based products, **supercritical carbon dioxide (CO2)** extraction is a common technique used among leading large-scale processors in the cannabis industry. This process requires high-tech equipment and a strong understanding of molecular compounds. CO2 extraction involves transitioning the compound from gas to liquid to supercritical in a series of steps within the machine involving pressure and temperature manipulation. Essentially, the compound is considered supercritical when it surpasses critical points in pressure and temperature, making it a form between gas and liquid. This supercritical form is then mixed with plant materials to separate compounds within the plant, in this case cannabinoids and terpenes. Next, the extracted mix passes through a separator that isolates each individual compound from each other as well as from the supercritical CO_2, which is ultimately recycled for repeat use. Scientists can extract different compounds by simply controlling the pressure and temperature of the solvent. While this is an increasingly popular methodology in cannabis, this is actually also the way mainstream manufacturers isolate plant compounds and create distillates for perfumes, oils and food additives. The isolation process allows for more versatility and exact chemical compound measurements in product development. More importantly, the process doesn't significantly alter the chemical composition of the extracted compounds and it doesn't leave behind unsafe residue as described with butane. Many scientists believe this is the cleanest, safest and most cost effective method of extraction in consumer manufactured goods.

Alcohol extraction is also an option and has become very popular among cancer patients who use highly concentrated **Rick Simpson's Oil (RSO)**. Through anecdotes and shared stories, RSO or whole plant oil is unofficially credited for reducing the growth of tumors and various cancer cells. Ethanol, or whole grain alcohol, is a good solvent for cannabinoid and terpene extraction. The process can be completed at room temperature using relatively simple equipment. The lower boiling point of ethanol also makes it a fairly easy solvent to remove. In fact, the original RSO extraction process was a completely home-based process initially which is why so many copycats have emerged in the market. That said, scaling for industrial level production is not too difficult with most concern around storage compliance because of how much is needed to produce the best results.

Recently, cannabis-specific laboratories using innovative extraction methods have emerged. BAS Research, for example, is a cannabis company combining innovative science with quad-tested protocols to produce cannabis extracts of exceptional quality, potency, consistency and safety. Companies like BAS provide contract services to a range of client companies that manufacture cannabis end products such as vape cartridges, edibles or topicals. Working with a contract manufacturer to supply extract oil gives these downstream production companies a competitive edge because of the higher quality, more consistency in their products generated and more accurate product analysis. In fact, BAS Research has capitalized on this need in the market by creating the first certification seal in the cannabis industry. Brands and products in the market sealed with BAS Infused™ are certified to be infused with cannabis oil that has gone through the rigorous standards required to meet the safety and purity thresholds of BAS Research products.

Cannabis processing and product manufacturing is growing rapidly, particularly with the federal legalization of hemp. If you're interested in crossing over into this sector of the industry, be sure to read up on traditional and modern forms of extraction as well as the latest trends. Entry into the extraction space involves getting licensed or working with a licensed entity because you are touching the plant. As mentioned previously, this can be complicated and expensive. Also, different states generally have different laws and regulations for high-potency extractions, with some states regulating the volume and accessibility of concentrated extracts in the legal market. I recommend you select a place to set up operations with access to high quality, inexpensive cannabis flower and a robust legal market with multiple licensing types. Immediately, Oregon comes to mind as an optimal market for new entrepreneurs willing to relocate to jump in the market.

For individuals with drive, capital and repeatable techniques as an extraction artist, this sector can be quite lucrative. Three years ago, vape pen sales represented only low single digits of overall cannabis product sale. Today, it has grown to almost 30% of the legal market and climbing. In terms of future growth opportunities, processing and extraction are extremely important steps in the supply chain for manufacturing infused products. Therefore, even as the popularity of vapes start to level out, extraction techniques will still be a very important input for final consumer products, including edibles and topicals.

30. Does your skill include processing or extraction within another industry? Is there a legal state where you can apply your expertise? How can you tailor the process uniquely to your set of skills?

```



```

31. What ideas, if any, could make processing or extraction run smoother or be more consistent in the cannabis industry?

```



```

32. Based on what you've learned so far, what can you think of that is missing in current processing and extraction methods or what do you think you can provide to elevate the industry?

```



```

Extraction

Right now, there are a plethora of cannabis products in virtually every market, from beverages to edibles, with more introduced every day. As indicated, many of these products are manufactured using cannabis extract as a primary input, each with its own flavor derived from terpene and cannabinoid profiles. Here are a few companies innovating in the space.

Moxie, a cannabis extract company founded in 2015, is a leader in the concentrated cannabis space. The company utilizes pharmaceutical level processes, laboratory testing and strict safety standards to ensure the quality of its products. They have state of the art production facilities in California and Pennsylvania, a recently legalized medical marijuana market. Other concentrate brands like Blue River™ Terpenes combine full spectrum terpenes and the latest solventless technologies to guarantee better ingredients and better product experiences. They have the largest assortment of *types* of solventless extracts to choose from, ranging from rosin to jelly sauce to their signature Blue River™ Flan™. While you pay a premium for their solventless extracts, the consumption experience is always worth it!

Cannabis Extract Types; Image courtesy of Cresco Cannabis

When extraction is complete, depending on the process used, the final concentrated substance can be converted into many different usable forms. The different extract forms have both technical and street names, depending on the market. From shatter to sauce, by and large, the terms are describing physical appearance and consistency of the concentrated extract. As you can imagine, cannabis oils can be difficult to transport and use. Extraction companies, like Moxie and Blue River™ Terps convert the oils into wax, shatter, budder, snap and pull, which are drier and easier-to-handle formats. For those interested in more isolated cannabinoid and terpene manufacturing, **cannabis distillate** is a commonly used, more purified and processed extract that removes all the residual plant material and separates the cannabinoid molecules. Typically used for downstream infusion and precise product formulation, distillates are odorless and tasteless, and can also be vaped. Although distillate can be created from most extract forms, supercritical fluid carbon dioxide extractions already isolate the compounds effectively, providing an excellent starting point for distillate formulation.

Extractions satisfy the need for a concentrated and more potent cannabis experience. If creating concentrates is your interest, make the necessary investment to truly learn the myriad of techniques, perfecting at least one. Take a hands-on class to learn how to make concentrates or the latest innovation in extraction technology. Immerse yourself fully, whether your goal is to start a multinational conglomerate or to work at a concentrate company. If you already have experience in manufacturing and product development, this may be a great place for you to jump into the market.

Bud & Bougie Denver 2019; Cannabis joints rolled in wax and kief

Infusion

Once cannabis has been extracted into the concentrated forms we described in the last section, there are many different types of manufactured goods for consumers to enjoy. The technique for combining concentrated forms of cannabis with a base formula is called infusion. Cannabis-infused products can generally be classified into three main sub-categories based on the physiological mechanism and consumer experience.

#1 Edibles

Edibles are the largest sub-category of the infusion market. Collectively, cannabis-infused foods, candies and beverages represent one of the fastest growing segments of the cannabis industry, both legal and illegal. Infused foods come in various forms, but many new entrants are still leveraging sweet, baked goods or traditional confections, such as chocolate.

Within the candy segment, gummies are still extremely popular despite recent child-protection laws in some states and countries, like Canada, preventing certain gummy shapes and look-alike brands. Wana Brands is a leading multi-state cannabis brand best known for infused sour gummies with consistent and accurate dosing. Although sweets and candies are still prevalent product types in the edibles market, we are seeing more innovation and sophistication beyond the days of "pot brownies" or "special" gummy bears. In fact, edible companies have played a large role in marketing to emerging consumer segments, particularly women, with industry-leading dosing, packaging, and branding. One such example is Kiva, a brand that produces delicious award-winning chocolate edibles and recently added a flavorful gummies product line gaining popularity in the California market. They entered the cannabis industry as experts in confections and have succeeded in crossing over that expertise into every product developed.

Finally, cannabis-infused gel capsules or pills, like those made by Prana, work in the body like other edibles but the consumer experience is more aligned with a traditional pharmaceutical. Although mentioned here, they are also part of the growing category of cannaceuticals, where cannabis meets biopharmaceutical practices and delivery mechanisms. These products are very precise in development to ensure that each pill or capsule has the exact same dosage each time and/or specialized formulation. We will talk more about the importance of cannaceuticals shortly.

Beverages represent one of the fastest growing segments of the edibles sub-category. The first cannabis-infused beverages were produced by Dixie Elixirs and these products were comparable to soft drinks. Infused coffees and teas, like the highly popular and women-owned Kikoko brand, are now available in developing markets. More recently, infused alcoholic beverages from beer to wine have emerged in the market and quickly gained traction in adult-use markets despite concern among pioneers in the industry from potential side effects.

No matter the edible type, there are still significant challenges globally with accurate and consistent dosing in this category. Within the illegal market, most product manufacturers do not have a strong understanding of food science and have little knowledge of their product potency. Without understanding how many milligrams of active ingredients, such as cannabinoids and terpenes, the producer can't provide the consumers with accurate dosage per serving size. Further, homemade edibles generally don't have the same consistency of cannabinoids throughout the entire product because of a lack of manufacturing process and uniformity required at a certified Good Manufacturing Process (cGMP) facility. Finally, there are no caps on dosages within the unregulated market, which means you can get edibles with more than 100 milligrams in one dose. This doesn't mean, however, that higher standards can't be achieved in an unregulated market particularly if consumers start to demand and expect more.

At present, consumers don't have enough education around edible consumption, including onset time and dosing levels. Most people are still working with a very limited understanding of what to expect from a cannabis edible experience outside of the stereotypical "super stoned" or "I almost died" experience. If you are thinking about operating an edible business in a developing and/or gray unregulated market, it is only a matter of time before that market becomes regulated. You can get ahead of the game by simply creating products that meet a minimum product viability (MVP) for the average consumer product experience with food, candies and beverages. Take the time to learn more about ingredient consistency, potency and dosage per serving size. Apply your learnings to your edible brand. If possible, you should test your product before going to market. Whether it is a small focus group of friends to test onset time and consistency, or partnering with a small lab to batch test your formula, ensuring consumer protection and developing brand trust should be a primary focus. Next time you are in a store, look at the packaging within the sub-category of your intended product. Note all of the ingredients shared along with the nutritional value panel.

Unfortunately, the legal market, depending on your state, is likely not that much better, with some states still seeing legal brands with inaccurate dosing on their packaging. In others, the standard deviation of error for product potency can be up to 15%! It is also very rare for a legal brand to indicate the extraction process they used for manufacturing their goods. This an important piece of information in consumer decision because the effects of the edible vary depending on if it was made with isolate, distillate or whole-plant extract. Isolates and distillates remove most everything except the cannabinoid of focus (usually THC or CBD) and therefore, these infused products typically do not have the modulating and entourage effects of terpenes, flavonoids and other cannabinoids found in whole-plant infusions. More advanced companies have begun to focus on distillate formulations that add back terpenes in order to recreate molecular profiles of common strains with desired effects.

#2 Topicals

These are cannabis-infused products designed for application directly on to the skin. Most topicals are active by way of the epithelium or the outer layers of cells surrounding the human body and can be an incredibly effective product category. There is actually an abundance of CB1 and CB2 receptors throughout the many layers of the skin along with the soft tissue just under the skin.[1] Cannabis-infused topicals are also very important for the cannabis industry because these products provide an approachable method of consumption for people unfamiliar with the wellness benefits of cannabis products. These products tend to do very well for populations that are 55 and older, particularly for managing pain due to inflammation, such as with arthritis. Generally, whether a topical contains THC or not, consumers do not have to worry about getting the "high" effect. Outside of transdermals, most topicals will not deliver enough THC to the bloodstream to feel a significant impact in the brain. The molecule will primarily remain caught up in the local receptors of the skin and soft-tissue just below.

If you reviewed the history of cannabis, you would find that topical application is one of the most widespread therapeutic uses for the plant globally. For example in Mexico, cannabis has been soaked in rubbing alcohol and used for treating muscle or joint ailments for centuries. Because of this understanding, I believe there is a huge business opportunity for people in both marijuana and hemp segments to keep expanding and innovating in the infused topicals sub-category. Similar to natural hair care products in the last 10 years, do-it-yourself (DIY) topical home remedies have been tremendously effective anecdotally. The only things savvy entrepreneurs really need to get started are the willingness to experiment and to perfect their products.

#3 Cannaceuticals - Sublinguals, Transdermals & More!

Cannaceuticals is an emerging subcategory of the infused and manufactured consumer products in the cannabis industry. As previously mentioned, this area of the market is where cannabis science meets biopharmaceutical practices. Cannaceutical products are made from isolated cannabinoid molecules with very precise distillation, formulation and dosing. This is the main reason I have separated this sub-category from edibles and topicals. **Real talk:** You can make infused edibles or topicals at home, but you can't make

---

[1] Del Rio, C. Millian, E., et al. (November 2018).The endocannabinoid system of the skin. A potential approach for the treatment of skin disorders. *Biochemical Pharmacology* (157), 122-133

cannaceutical products without a professional laboratory environment.

Within the United States, this portion of the market is fairly small but rapidly growing. However, the biggest strides in cannaceuticals have come from the global markets where cannabis science is more readily studied and researched by credentialed professionals. Tilray, a Canadian pharmaceutical and cannabis company, became the first medical cannabis producer in North America to become GMP certified in 2016 and now has global operations spanning Portugal, Germany, Australia and Latin America. The company is actively involved in multiple clinical trials across the globe, ranging from the effects of treatment on post-traumatic stress disorder (PTSD) in partnership with New York University to trials in Spain on the tolerability of cannabis treatment for glioblastomas, an aggressive type of brain tumor. Most recently, they made history by being the first cannabis company to conduct an Initial Public Offering (IPO) on the NASDAQ. Their rapid global success highlights the growing interest of the scientific research and medical education communities around the world regarding cannabis as a medicinal, active ingredient. Because of this, we have more and more companies coming to the table with this same model and thought process, thereby increasing the different types of of cannaceuticals on the market.

Cannaceuticals are generally delivered to consumers in the form of pills or capsules. Once in the body, these products function similarly to edibles in that the active ingredients are absorbed in the gastrointestinal tract. Many companies entering the market here are bringing well-known pharmaceutical technology, such as extended-release, rapid release or nanotechnology, to impact the absorption and bioavailability of the active ingredients. Depending on the market, cannabinoid dosages can range from 5mgs per pill to 50mgs per pill. Most companies are focused on activated forms of THC and CBD, providing variations in formulaic ratios of the two molecules. However, there are a few companies that have started offering cannaceuticals featuring other cannabinoids like CBG or the acidic, non-active versions such as THC-A.
One step further, products are coming to market with formulations including other beneficial ingredients, such as plant-derived terpenes and melatonin.

Sublinguals are the second largest sub-category within cannaceuticals, most commonly delivered in the form of oil or alcohol-based cannabinoid tinctures similar to Rick Simpson's Oil (RSO). Drops of the highly potent tincture are placed under the tongue using a dropper or more commonly, a syringe. At the site of contact, cannabinoids and other compounds pass through the oral mucosa into the bloodstream. This delivery mechanism is also referred to as transmucosal and believe it or not, is a similar mechanism for infused buccal lozenges or rectal suppositories. When consumed this way, the onset of effects can be relatively short, ranging from 5 to 10 minutes with a gradual increase over time until the full dosage has been delivered. In other words, it doesn't hit you with everything in the first 5 minutes but as the lozenge melts or as the tincture sits in the gum tissue under the tongue, more cannabinoids are delivered to the body. Unless, of course, the tincture is swallowed rather than held under the tongue. In that case, onset of effects will be more like an edible which is considerably slower. Because tinctures can be a messy and occasionally uncertain sublingual, we have started to see an increase in more sublingual strips in the legal cannabis market. For example, brands like CannaStrips™ provide cannabinoid and terpene infused strips that deliver a consistent dosage every time as the strip dissolves into the gum or cheek tissue. Certainly the strips can be accidentally swallowed as well, but there is a lower rate of error as compared to liquid tinctures.

Transdermal patches or pens are examples of *specialized* topicals that are created with technology allowing the tiny cannabinoid molecules to travel transdermally or across the skin to enter the blood directly. Because skin is an effective protective barrier, transdermal products generally work best when applied to the thinnest and most venous areas of the skin, such as the inside wrist or top of the foot. This variation in the technology and mechanisms for cannabinoid delivery makes a world of difference in the overall consumer experience due to onset time and the cannabinoid bioavailability. As mentioned before, a product that delivers more directly into the blood will have a faster onset and higher bioavailability than one that must travel through many layers of skin cells and soft tissue. One of the most popular brands of transdermal patches and pens in the legal cannabis market is made by Mary's Medicinals™. They have a wide assortment due to their industry leadership in cannabinoid product formulation, which we will talk about further in our next section.

Finally, as more biopharmaceutical technology is applied to the industry, there have been more attempts to bring new products to market with this foundation. A few examples include cannabinoid inhalers, infused suppositories and infused nasal sprays. The goal is to leverage the insights from consumer behaviors with these delivery mechanisms to create a product that is easily adoptable by mainstream consumers, and likely more discreet and more consistent than just smoking a joint.

33. Do you have experience in food, beverage or cosmetic manufacturing? If so, how can you incorporate your experience into cannabis? Provide at least 3 ways.

34. Are you a chef or caterer? Do you own a restaurant, coffee shop, or any other establishments serving food? If yes, how might you incorporate cannabis into your current business? Name 3 ways.

35. Are you a DIY guru for personal care products? Or do you have your own beauty brand (hair, skin, nails) already? If yes, what are 3 steps you can take to capitalize on cannabis as an important ingredient?

Scientific discovery and innovation in the cannabis industry has led to a robust formulation subcategory. Cannabis is comprised of between 65 to 400 unique chemical compounds. Each has specific individual effects on the human body and mind. There are also major implications to modulating and entourage effects of combinations of these chemical compounds. Formulation is the art and science of identifying these different compounds, putting together cannabinoids and expressing other active chemicals to achieve a distinct result on efficacy. People who've worked with the plant have always understood that different strains of cannabis have varying effects on the human body, but initially didn't know why, and certainly didn't understand how to fully manipulate those effects.

> "*Formulation* is the science of putting together cannabinoids and other active chemicals to achieve a distinct result on efficacy."

The advent of specialized analytical equipment to test cannabis, and the ability to do it relatively cheaply and quickly helps the industry understand both the different compound profiles of each strain and ways to manipulate the profile to fulfill specific consumer needs. For example, based on a limited understanding of the relationship between tetrahydrocannabinol (THC) and cannabidiol (CBD) in the body, many companies are now focused on creating formulaic variations in the CBD to THC (CBD:THC) ratio.

Formulation Innovation

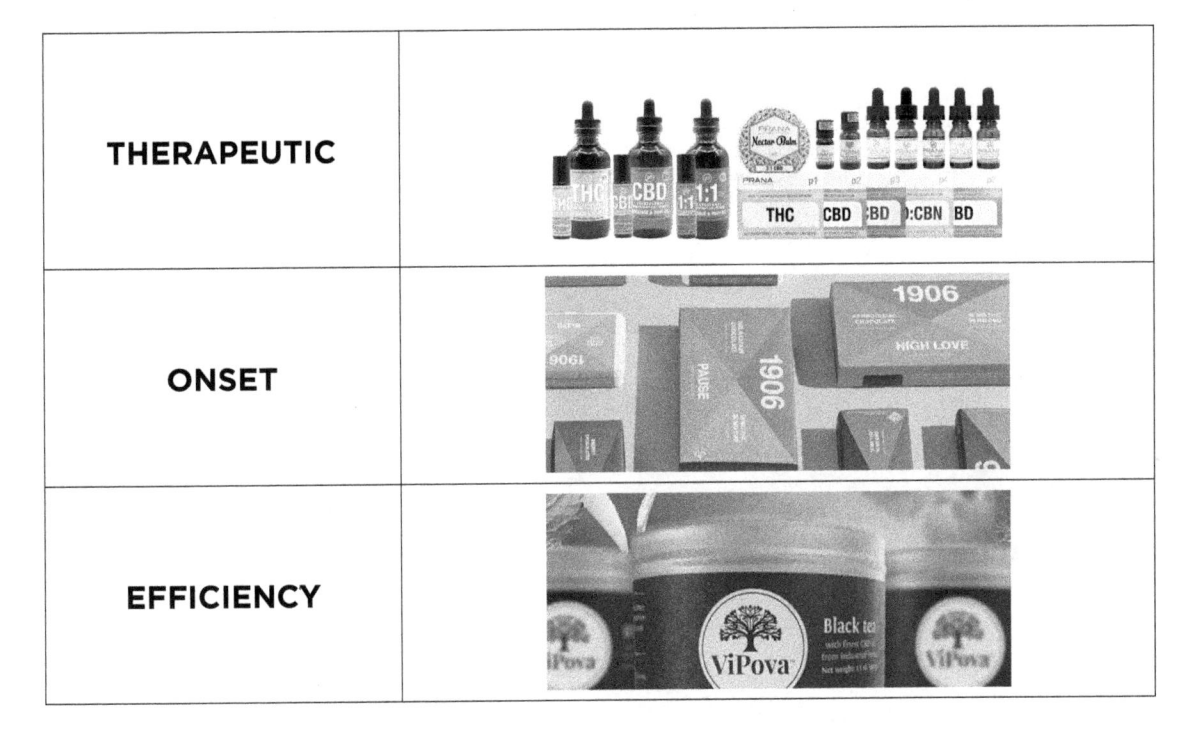

THERAPEUTIC	
ONSET	
EFFICIENCY	

Cannabis formulation for infused products is led by research driven innovation. Companies like Prana and Aunt Zelda's produce plant-based medicines with distinct cannabinoid profiles targeting different medical conditions. Ebbu, which was recently purchased for $19 million by Canopy Growth, is editing and examining the cannabis genome, ultimately restructuring the plant on a cellular level using modern technology. And, 1906, which was founded by a fellow Princeton tiger, has developed a rapid activation edible using a technique to significantly reduce onset time of cannabis. Generally, it takes about 45 minutes for a user to feel the effects after ingesting a cannabis-infused product. This brand boasts products with an onset time of 20 minutes or less. ViPova™ Tea credits its patented DehydraTECH™ technology for the enhanced bioavailability of its CBD infused tea, allowing the company to use less CBD in their products, and still maintain a positive effect on the human body.

These companies are on the cutting edge of cannabis and technology. Innovative entrepreneurs interested in this space should read up on the latest infusion technology and figure out how it can be applied in the cannabis space. They can also leverage age-old methods to formulate more traditional products such as edibles and topicals that have been used for centuries.

36. Do you have the skills and interest necessary to explore formulation? How can you enter the sector? What would your process be?

37. What can you formulate to make a distinct product in this sector?

38. How can you improve the formulation process? Can you change the process to produce a unique product?

Delivery Mechanisms

Delivery mechanisms are experiencing explosive growth as consumption methods have become far more sophisticated than just smoking a joint. This sector specializes in devices and emerging mechanisms that can be used to consume cannabis. There have been a number of notable breakthroughs in the past decade. In this area, vaporizers, which gently heat cannabis to release activated (decarboxylated) cannabinoids, specifically THC, without burning or combustion have arguably had the greatest impact. Vaping virtually eliminates the risk of creating carcinogenic smoke while consuming cannabis. In the past, vaporizers were bulky, expensive and difficult to use. While much more streamlined, today's high end vapes can cost more than a thousand dollars! Our team office readily uses Puffco's high end vaporizer, The Peak which retails at over $300. Truthfully, these price points have made them out of reach for the average cannabis consumer, until the entry of more reasonably priced models into the market.

Vape pens or cartridges, which can be purchased for less than $100, have become immensely popular as they allow people to use cannabis easily and discreetly, without the discomfort or smell of smoking. The traditional method requires consumers to grind their weed, roll it into a joint, and light it, creating smoke, odor and ash. Vape cartridges, by comparison, are filled with cannabis extract which is then heated by an electrical mechanism to create a cloud of vapor infused with cannabinoids, terpenes and any other molecules within the extract. One of my favorite vape brands, James

Henry SF, formulates with medical doctors to develop reliable and effective vape products. Based in California, this Black-owned cannabis vape company focuses their product line on unique cannabinoid and terpene combinations that can be used for various moods from Daytime Focus CBD to Social Sativa to Retreat Indica.

However explosive this segment of the market has been, this relatively new portable vaporizer technology continues to evolve and there is still much room for improvement. Early in the rise of popularity, waste became a persistent issue. Whether the vape pen is fully disposable or just the cartridge, a moderate cannabis user can rack up quite a bit of plastic and metal post-consumption. There are very few, if any, recycle programs for disposable vape pens. However, there has been an increase in the number of refillable vape cartridges, although this is simply robbing Peter to pay Paul because the refills come in plastic syringes which can also accumulate over time without a formal vape cartridge recycling program.

The biggest risks currently and by far with this delivery mechanism are surrounding testing in the legal market and counterfeiting with the illegal market. For example, as California transitioned into an adult-use legal market, it increased testing requirements for vape pens to include heavy metal testing. With the strictest testing in the country, the California cannabis industry uncovered many vape cartridge brands testing positive for toxic, heavy metals including lead! Typically, heavy metal contamination of cannabis products, if found, is due to cross-contamination in processing and/or from the plants absorption of metals from the soil during cultivation. However, for vape products, the heavy metal contamination seems to be driven by the metal used for the electrical heating units, mostly made in China, where it is common to add very small amounts of lead to make the metal more moldable. Although China factories follow pretty strict compliance laws, this is not translating to below the threshold set for the legal cannabis industry in California.

That said, the heavy metals in vape cartridges are going undetected in other states, which doesn't create global consumer confidence in the delivery mechanism that is supposed to be a better alternative to smoking. The most common type of vape cartridge used by brands in the cannabis industry is CCELL, which tested better than other vape pen technology on the market but were still failing the California testing. Completely removing the risk of lead contamination from the metal components will require a change in product development of the apparatus in China. Given the size of the California market, this has sparked a sense of urgency for these updates by cannabis brands using CCELL technology.

Within the illegal market, there has been an increase in counterfeiting known legal brands, particularly within the vape pen segment of the market. Thanks to online access to marketing collateral such as logos and the ease of securing empty CCELL vapes via China, it isn't difficult to make bootleg or counterfeit cannabis vape products. First off, it helps that many legal cannabis companies still have remedial packaging and marketing, which is easily replicated. In these cases, counterfeiters are making their own cannabis oils and using the branding of the legitimate brand presumably to sell more vapes "piggybacking" their credibility. Sadly, it is also the case that legitimate and licensed cannabis companies are selling their own failed vape products in the illegal market. More recently a major cannabis brand was busted preparing to distribute over $20 million in illegal, untested merchandise, specifically vape cartridges.

While vape pens have been the fastest growing segment in the cannabis market for the last few years, I predict this segment will slow in growth as we stumble through understanding the technology and the testing to keep consumers safe. If you are interested in crossing over into the market in this segment, I would suggest consulting a vape technologist, like Arnaud Dumas de Rauly, CEO of The Blinc Group and Chairman of International Organization for Standardization (ISO) Standards for vape products. In his roles, he is a thought leader on vape technology safety and regulation globally developing best in class cannabis vaping hardware and complementary ancillary products. Given the climate of concern, I would also recommend staying away from this segment unless you are supported by processing and product development excellence, from knowhow to facilities. We are regularly uncovering new information regarding health benefits and hazards of vaping which makes for a risky business venture in a confusing market. And, as a general rule of thumb, I don't recommend consumption from the illegal market, whether it's homemade or a top brand.

We have already covered the other delivery mechanisms on the rise in the legal cannabis industry. Certainly, this is an area of the market with white space for innovation and worthy of a quick recap. As previously mentioned, transdermal skin patches are an emerging new format for cannabis delivery. Mary's Medicinals transdermal skin patches are industry leaders, dispensing cannabinoids and other molecules through the blood vessels and providing 8 to 12 hours of relief with various formulations. Buccal lozenges and sublingual strips are another emerging form of cannabis transmucosal delivery. The lozenges or strips can be placed between the cheek and teeth or under the tongue. Both will gradually melt into the gum tissue or oral mucosa. Delivery via this mechanism bypasses the digestive system, and unlike typical edibles or gummies, users will start feeling the effects in about 10 minutes. There are now cannabis-infused suppositories. This may come as a surprise, but suppositories are the single most efficient way of cannabinoid consumption. In a similar transmucosal mechanism, suppositories interact with the rectal mucosa which is rich in blood vessels. If users can overcome the discomfort, they offer the biggest bang for the buck. Although still fairly uncommon, nasal sprays, powders and water-soluble cannabinoid products have also entered the market. If manufactured well, all can offer consumers more ease of consumption and/or bioavailability.

39. Vape pens have become increasingly popular. How would you innovate or improve upon this delivery format, or *create an alternative*? How would you address the recent contamination and counterfeiting issue?

40. Do you have any experience with vape technology and consumer products within the e-cigarette market? How could you utilize that experience to make an impact in the legal cannabis industry?

41. Do you have any previous experience in product development and/or sourcing? How might you apply those skills to some of the challenges in popular delivery mechanisms? How would you innovate in this sector?

www.theweedhead.com

HEMP:
CBD Products & More

Hemp is cannabis. People are often surprised by this short, yet powerful fact. Although hemp and marijuana are part of the same scientific genus, they are regulated by global governments very differently. The major difference between hemp and marijuana is defined by the government and pertains to the level of tetrahydrocannabinol (THC). Hemp has virtually no trace of THC, specifically must be less than 0.3%.

In the United States, cannabis prohibition outlawed both hemp and marjuana for nearly a century. In 1937, the Marijuana Tax Act banned hemp production in the United States. After a lurid national propaganda campaign against the "devil's lettuce," the statute effectively also criminalized marijuana, restricting possession of the plant to individuals who paid an excise tax for certain authorized medical and industrial uses. We now know that these federal laws were not passed for the protection of U.S. citizens but rather for the protection of U.S. big businesses, such as petrochemical companies like DuPont and timber/paper companies like Hearst. Many believe it was in fact the industrial potential of hemp that sparked the prohibition of cannabis and marijuana was only used as the public scapegoat with all of the promoted "reefer madness" concerns.

Throughout the years, because of prohibition, hemp has remained relatively obscure as an agricultural or industrial crop in America. On February 7, 2014, this obscurity began to change, as President Obama signed the Farm Bill Act of 2013 into law. Section 7606 of the act, Legitimacy of Industrial Hemp Research, defines industrial hemp as distinct from marijuana, specifically focusing on industrial hemp having less than 0.3% THC concentration. It also authorized institutions of higher education or state departments of agriculture in states that legalized hemp cultivation to regulate and conduct hemp research and pilot programs. With nearly non-existent levels of THC, hemp, as defined by the U.S. government, is a non-intoxicating, genetically distinct variety of the plant *Cannabis sativa.*

On April 12, 2018, Senate Majority Leader Mitch McConnell (R-KY) introduced The Hemp Farming Act of 2018. The historic bill removes hemp completely from the Controlled Substances Act and regulates the plant as an agricultural crop. It also defines hemp as cannabis with 0.3% THC or less by dry weight and the bill allows states to regulate commercial hemp farming after submitting a plan to regulate it to the USDA. The bill authorizes crop insurance for hemp and provides funding for hemp research. Probably most important to the cannabis consumer market, the bill also defines hemp more broadly than the previous Farm Bill and now explicitly *includes* extracts and cannabinoids, such as cannabidiol (CBD), derived from the hemp plant. The President signed this into federal law with the 2018 Farm Bill in late December 2018, effectively making hemp and hemp-derived CBD products federally legal. It is important to point out that marijuana-derived CBD is still federally illegal, despite its identical molecular structure to hemp-derived CBD. **Real talk:** CBD as an isolated molecule functions the same way in the endocannabinoid system, regardless of whether it is marijuana- or hemp-derived. Eventually, I believe our hemp and marijuana laws will converge to align with the real science.

Nonetheless, this new law has been a game changer for the global cannabis industry because it means the United States will be looking to invest and capitalize quickly, going from the largest global importer of **hemp seeds** and fibers from China, Canada and Europe to a global producer and distributor. Furthermore, because CBD is illegal in Canada, we are seeing the big Canadian investors look to America for expansion opportunities. For example, Canopy Growth, a massive Canadian cannabis conglomerate known as the "Wal-Mart of weed", quickly moved into the U.S. hemp market transforming an old New York plant into an industrial hemp processing facility with plans to develop the surrounding land into a hemp industrial park for entrepreneurs interested in the emerging CBD market.

> ## "Not all parts of the hemp plant are created equal as it pertains to cannabinoid concentration."

Hemp is the long money because there are fewer barriers to entry and so many end uses for this plant. Structurally, like most plants, hemp can be broken into 4 parts: seeds, roots, stalks and leaves. For many years, we have been familiar with the dietary and cosmetic benefits of hemp seeds and hemp seed oil. Many people consider hemp seed a superfood. While it is rich in protein, fiber and omega-3 fatty acids, hemp seeds have little to no cannabinoids, specifically no CBD. Therefore, it can't be used for cannabinoid extraction and hemp seed oil will not provide the same benefits as CBD oil. This is a very important detail that is often overlooked by new entrants to the cannabis industry and a common rookie mistake. Hemp seed can be transformed into oil, flour, and fuel, but not all parts of the cannabis plant are created equal as it pertains to cannabinoid concentration.

Hemp root is a portion of the plant that is usually ignored, despite its historical importance as a medicine. Thousands of years ago, **cannabis root** was utilized to treat a range of ailments from inflammation to skin disorders to infections, a practice that continues in some parts of the world. Processed via boiling or juicing, hemp root is usually administered as a topical, contains little to no cannabinoids and are rich in triterpinoids, which are compounds with significant anti-inflammatory activity.

Looking next at stalks, this is where hemp and marijuana can often have the biggest physical differences in appearance. **Hemp stalk** is highly fibrous and can be grown up to 18 feet tall, if cultivated under the right conditions. This portion of the plant is used for industrialized products such as paper, plastic, rope, canvas and other fabrics. The stalk is arguably the most versatile component of the plant and is the key to making agriculture sexy again! From batteries to clothes to concrete, hemp stalk certainly is the "long" in the long money. Not only can the stalk be transformed into a vast array of products, we also know these hemp-based products are demonstrably sustainable and environmentally friendly. Hemp stalk usually does contain very small concentrations of cannabinoids, but likely not the best starting material for extraction.

Last but certainly not least, **hemp leaves** and flowers are often the first thing we think about when we consider the cannabis plant. Once trimmed and processed, hemp flower is nearly indistinguishable from marijuana flower. Furthermore, extraction and manufacturing of hemp flower to develop cannabinoid-infused products follows similar operational processes as marijuana flower extraction. However, unlike marijuana, the cannabinoid of highest abundance in hemp is cannabidiol (CBD). Therefore, hemp flower is the best starting material to extract and isolate CBD. Similar to marijuana, hemp extracts can be whole plant or full spectrum, including terpenes and other cannabinoids. However, with whole plant extracts, there is always risk that consumption can lead to a positive THC test because hemp still contains THC, albeit a very tiny amount (<0.3%). As a result, more and more, we are seeing the market move toward using CBD isolate as the main ingredient for infused product development. This ensures manufacturers can develop a product with 0% THC, which increases relative safety in the market for distribution and the ability for the company to market the product as such.

In 2014, we essentially relaunched the hemp industry in the United States and by 2018, we had over 25,000 acres of hemp growing in the country in the key states of Colorado, Oregon, North Dakota and Kentucky. This represents a nearly 300% increase to the 9,000 acres of hemp grown in 2016. Fast forward to 2019. The market is exploding with some states having 1000%+ growth in acres of hemp cultivation and number of hemp licenses secured. According to New Frontier Data, over 16,000 hemp licenses have been issued in 2019 for growing and processing. Tennessee, South Carolina and North Carolina have emerged quickly as contenders in hemp farming, extraction and manufacturing. With all of this growing in the United States, over 50% of the new licenses are being used for CBD-related product development. According to *Hemp Industry Journal*, the U.S. hemp industry will grow to $1.9 billion by 2022 with an estimated compound annual growth rate (CAGR) of nearly 15%. Approximately 35% or over $600 million will be due to CBD-based products.

Rather than being able to rapidly expand business and capitalize on the legacy built in the market, multiple cannabis companies including industry pioneer, Charlotte's Web, were sent cease and desist letters from the FDA for CBD-related efficacy claim violations. In some cases, the FDA removed products from the shelves and/or confiscated products due to these violations. At the same time, the FDA also issued multiple statements indicating their newfound interest and intention in regulating CBD-infused products, particularly ingestibles. In fact, they used their 2018 approval of GW Pharma's Epidiolex, the first FDA-approved CBD product, as precedent for why CBD should be regulated by the FDA. Due to the FDA's response after the passing of the 2018 Farm Bill, a few states including New York have placed restrictions on marketing and selling CBD-infused foods and edibles. These moves by the FDA pose a risk to developing brands in hemp-derived CBD natural products.

New brands must invest in FDA-compliant manufacturing partners or facilities and hire a good marketing lead, who understands the best practices for making product efficacy claims and necessary FDA packaging and e-commerce disclaimers. I would also recommend either staying away from ingestible products to avoid FDA scrutiny, or planning to spend $80-$100K on the testing necessary for FDA approval. While FDA approval is only a recommendation for product development and largely avoided by most consumer packaged goods (CPG) manufacturers, larger cannabis players will need to ensure all boxes are checked to avoid the agency's crosshairs. Smaller cannabis brands may be able to hide under the radar but eventually, dealing with the FDA is something every cannabis brand must consider in its growth strategy. If you have any prior experience working in FDA-approved manufacturing and compliant operations, your expertise may mean the difference between success and failure for a growing CBD company.

Much like marijuana, hemp flower can come in a variety of strains with different cannabinoid levels and terpene profiles. One such strain, CW2A, developed by industry pioneer, Charlotte's Web, recently became the first hemp strain to be awarded a U.S. patent on its unique genetics, capable of producing plants with over 6% of CBD and 0.27% THC. The plant patent gives Charlotte's Web protection from competitors growing that specific strain or cultivar from a clone. In 2020, the company is likely to also receive a utility patent which protects the seeds and chemical composition of the plant. The latter provides a wider range of protection. However, given the strain's ability to produce high quantities of dry weight CBD and the use of clones to start nurseries, this initial patent is a real business chess move to create a considerable competitive advantage for the company. For example, they now have a unique ability to drive revenue from royalties on their patent-protected strain, particularly from competitive companies like GW Pharma that need high-CBD hemp strains to manufacturer finished products.

If you are interested in either starting your own or investing in a CBD business, the information provided in this chapter is a foundation for you to build on. To grow, cultivate, and process hemp, most states require a license which can be acquired via application to the state agricultural or health departments. Think outside of the box for where you might want to obtain a license. Many states offer hemp license applications for fees as little as $100 to $500 dollars, which is far less than the fees associated with marijuana licensing. While the license application process may be cheaper and less arduous, the biggest barrier of entry to overcome is acquisition of the land, property and/or equipment necessary to cultivate, process or manufacture. For example, New York state's hemp licensing application is only $500 but land values continue to be among the highest in the country. Meanwhile, states like Oklahoma, North Carolina, Tennessee and Alabama are likely to have comparable application fees but far less cost of land or property.

If cultivating and manufacturing is not your interest or expertise, I would encourage potential entrepreneurs to consider becoming a wholesale distribution partner with established CBD brands. This is the least risky entrance into the CBD market and frankly, one of the best ways to transition from an illegal cannabis distributor into a legal market. If you are already "the plug" or local cannabis contact, odds are you have customers who have asked you about CBD. This is your opportunity to capitalize on the trust built in your relationships and the reach of your distribution network. Leveraging information you have learned here, you should be able to identify CBD brands and products worth selling in person or online. CBD marketplaces are a white space opportunity, especially if yours can help consumers sort through the seemingly countless new CBD products on the market. Holmes Organics is a minority-owned, hemp-derived CBD line offering budding entrepreneurs an entrance into the market via their independent sales opportunities. Ranging from tinctures to balms to pet treats, their oil goes through proprietary nanoemulsion process that produces smaller particles allowing for easier and faster absorption in the body.

If you choose to enter the market as a hemp-derived CBD product distributor, I would suggest onboarding a limited number of brands at a time, testing products yourself to speak to potency and effects. Be sure to collect certificates of analysis (COA) to pass along to consumers interested in knowing more about the molecular profile of the product. Often, it is best to target a specific audience with your assortment rather than try to be all to everyone. Curate and filter products based on your understanding of your target's needs and wants. For example, if your target market consists of 40-55 year old, former elite athletes, you may want to curate an assortment of products focused on helping with muscle pain and acute inflammation. CBD vapes, gummies and oil tinctures are the three most common product types, regardless of age group. So, you may want to consider starting off with 1-2 products for each type. When developing your assortment, I would also recommend pricing stratification to have at least a low-cost and medium-cost option for each type. The price difference may be driven by size/quantity or quality or potency. If you choose to sell online, be sure to utilize approved branded collateral and copy, with particular focus on eliminating any perceived efficacy claims. Believe it or not, even when third party distributors or consumers make public claims about a brand's efficacy, it is still the brand's responsibility according to the FDA. Therefore, try not to add any superfluous copy to the product descriptions and if necessary, hire a product copywriter to assist.

Finally, regardless of how you enter the hemp sector, don't overlook other cannabinoids or terpenes that can be derived legally from hemp. As the plant's power is revealed, we are learning more about the benefits of each of these unique compounds. For example, cannabigerol (CBG) has shown promising medicinal benefits in early studies because it is a vasodilator (increases the size of blood vessels by relaxing smooth muscle) and has neuroprotective capabilities. Because of this, cannabinoid scientists are examining CBG's effects on glaucoma, neurodegenerative diseases and bladder dysfunction. Undoubtedly, this is an exciting time to join the cannabis industry and as you continue with the workbook, please remember that most things discussed in this book apply fairly equally across marijuana and hemp. Although hemp may not be as sexy as marijuana, its impact to the global market across multiple industries will be much more profitable and mainstream in reach. If you are considering a plant-touching business, it is in your best interest to enter the market with the lowest barrier (hemp) and leverage the capital and know-how to infiltrate more difficult markets (marijuana).

42. What are some of the major differences between Hemp and Marijuana?

HINT: Include both physical and regulatory differences

43. If you have an ancillary business idea, how might that idea be applied to the Hemp sector of the market?

44. Do you already have an established network of customers? How might you introduce credible CBD products to your network? What are some of the key tools that would be necessary? Digital and In-Person?

VETERINARY & PETS

Every living creature on the planet, with the exception of insects, has an endocannabinoid system. This includes the pets we have at home. Not surprisingly, because of this fact, a number of veterinary health issues respond incredibly well to cannabis. In fact, cannabis-infused veterinary products are turning up increasingly on retail shelves, including options like medicated doggy treats and pet-specific tinctures. Basically, every product type we can think of humans can be made for our four-legged family and pet owners are more likely to try ingestible products on their pets before themselves. That's why this sector of the market is fast growing and currently boasts more innovative product development than its comparable human category.

I would be remiss if I didn't include my own story of successfully using cannabinoid treatment for a family pet. Shortly after moving to Arizona, our family dog, a loving and loyal 6 year old pit named Tonka, began to experience occasional bouts of extreme coughing. These episodes seemed random and scary because he would often pass out from the physical exertion of the coughing. While rubbing on him one day, I found a medium-sized lump behind his ear and we quickly took Tonka to the vet for further investigation. As it turns out, this lump was a mast cell tumor and Tonka was suffering from Mast Cell Disease in his lungs causing him to cough uncontrollably.

Mast cells are important immune cells that help us build immune tolerance and fight foreign pathogen infiltration by releasing granules of histamine into the affected area. While this is helpful when functioning normally, mast cell disorders can also cause severe allergic reactions due to the excess histamine released in the body. In the case of Tonka, he was having trouble breathing because large amounts of active mast cells had infiltrated more than half of his lungs. The vet was very supportive and provided us end of life options, predicting Tonka would have less than 6 months to live given his age. Although he was not a good candidate for surgery to remove the lump, she indicated that we could get "more time and less coughing" if we gave Tonka daily treatments with Benadryl or an antihistamine to offset what was being produced in his lungs due to the disease. We took her advice, but we also added a daily regimen of cannabinoid treatment in the form of a high-potency, whole plant tincture.

Nearly 4 years later, Tonka is 10 years old, still alive and doing well! Beyond his miraculous survival, we also noticed a few other changes in Tonka with cannabis in his diet. The lump eventually got smaller and is now nearly non-existent. And, unlike previous experiences, Tonka became a willing participant in receiving his daily cannabinoid treatments as if he knew it was helping. During the first 6 months, with the higher dosages, Tonka slept more often and he wasn't as easily agitated or excited (except for the occasional doorbell). Today, we just maintain him on a daily CBD supplement and lots of love!

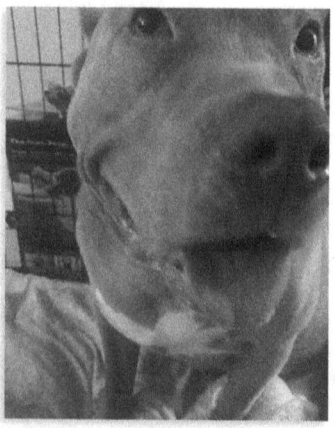

Tonka, alive & well, after cannabinoid treatments.

45. Are you a veterinarian and/or do you work in the pet industry (retail, kennel, concierge)? If so, how might you apply your knowhow and experience into the developing cannabis industry?

46. What are some common products in animal wellness that would benefit from cannabis infusion?

47. Are there some techniques that are used in treating animals that you can improve on using cannabis?

PACKAGING

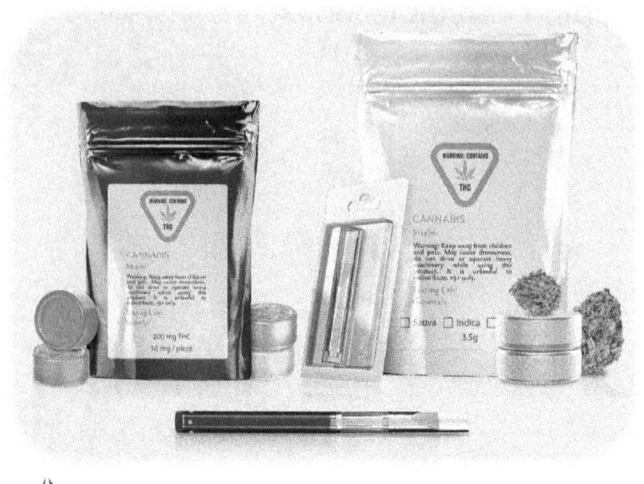

Packaging is yet another area with huge potential. As an ancillary or non-plant touching business, this sector doesn't face the same level of federal scrutiny as other businesses. For most of us, cannabis packaging has always meant plastic baggies (the dime bag) or old film roll containers (8th or larger). Packaging did not get much better when the medical cannabis industry started in California over 20 years ago. However, step into most cannabis dispensaries now, and you'll see how packaging has evolved, with emphasis on both presentation as well as functionality.

There is a whole range of white space opportunities to explore under the packaging category. One potential niche involves coming up with packaging for individual, delicate, living cannabis clones to facilitate transportation. This is a big challenge as the transport journey can sometimes take up to 4 or 8 hours and involve difficult climate conditions. Specialized packaging has to help the clone withstand the journey. Another, involves coming up with eco-friendly packaging. The cannabis community places a high value on sustainability and protecting mother nature. However, most cannabis packaging is neither sustainable nor eco-friendly. More often than not, this is due to the legal requirements. For example, some states require packaging flower in units no larger than eighth (1/8) of an ounce. But what happens when you want to purchase a quarter or half or more? You probably guessed, the consumer is allowed to buy more but given multiple eighths to equal the value of the purchase. So, if you purchased a half (1/2) ounce of a strain, you would leave with FOUR containers with an eighth ounce.

Childproof packaging is also experiencing rapid growth. This is because U.S. states and other legal jurisdictions mandate that cannabis be sold in child-resistant packaging. Generally, this packaging is unflattering and conspicuous. Inventing a form of childproof cannabis packaging that does not destroy the marketability of the product is the industry's equivalent of building a better mousetrap. The distinct odor of cannabis presents another opportunity for evolution. Many people aren't comfortable with the strong smell of terpenes lingering on them as they carry their stash around, which makes it a great niche for innovation. In fact, there are a number of products developed to counter this issue, like smell-proof plastic bags, as well as women's purses and handbags equipped with smell-proof technology and childproof locks. Currently, our marketplace sells Erbanna bags, which are stylish and functional odor-blocking handbags and backpacks. In fact, I never leave home without my Mindy or Kimberly bag, which will hold my pipe and flower containers.

Cannabis must be transported in massive quantities for processing, presenting another packaging opportunity. The harvested plants are moved from grower to the extractor and from the extractor to the manufacturer. How does one put twenty five gallons of extremely viscous cannabis oil into a container, so that it can be transported and emptied in a way that ensures achieving maximum yield and little to no waste? Silicone concentrate or extract carriers have become the go-to solution for both large size and small scale cannabis oil packaging in recent years. Cannabis extracts are often sticky, and if you put them in glass or plastic, you will end up wasting a lot of extract because you will not be able to remove from the container. However, it peels right off silicone, so these silicone vials and containers for extracts have become hugely popular.

Travel friendly packaging also represents a huge opportunity. Cannabis consumer friendly laws are still relatively rare. Many cannabis patients travel between friendly and unfriendly environments, and discreet packaging could mean the difference between access and arrest. Please note, I am in no way advocating for transporting cannabis into illegal environments. Consumers do so at their own risk. However, I am suggesting there are massive business opportunities for industrial engineers and/or sourcing specialists that can find or develop packaging that resolves some of these issues in the legal cannabis industry because consumers will likely utilize them.

Kushco Holdings (ticker: KHSB) is probably the largest cannabis-focused packaging company in the world with over $100 million in annual sales. There are also a few mainstream packaging companies, like Contempo Packaging, adding verticals that focus specifically on compliant cannabis packaging. Delving into this sector as an entrepreneur requires a background in design and partnership with a qualified packaging manufacturer, or starting your own manufacturing unit. Costs for entry can add up, so be prepared for a significant financial investment as you develop or buy your inventory. However, the potential upside is huge because cannabis companies, specifically ones focused on marijuana, will always need compliant cannabis packaging.

48. What are some of your packaging ideas that can address the unique needs of cannabis listed above? Name at least 2 ideas.

> *Hint: Three most important cannabis packaging needs are safety, quality and sustainability.*

49. Do you have previous experience in packaging, bottling or other consumer products? How can you put your know how to use in the packaging sector?

50. What other industries might offer innovative packaging solutions for the cannabis industry? Name at least 2 and why.

StartSMART Coalition - NY State Lobby Day 2018

SOFTWARE & INFORMATION TECHNOLOGY

There is a tremendous demand for software and IT in the cannabis industry, and plenty of room for new people to get involved. The first industry specific products here were one-size-fits-all point of sale systems like BioTrack and MJ Freeway.

Now, cannatech offerings have expanded to incorporate ordering platforms that connect consumers with dispensaries, as well as the development of social media platforms that connect cannabis aficionados, creating a social environment for them to engage. New brands such as Jade Insights and CannaTrax (C-Trax) have emerged to provide more refined and customized business intelligence solutions at point of sale. C-Trax is currently the only cannabis POS and inventory technology with full integration with Square payments. This is particularly important as most payment processors have begun to shut down cannabis-affiliated businesses, even if they don't sell cannabis. In addition, there are various delivery apps and digital marketplaces that have also emerged in both legal and illegal markets.

For those interested in Business-to-Business (B2B) transactions, trading platforms function almost like commodities exchanges. Companies like Americanex and Cannabis Hemp Exchange (CHEX) provide platforms where wholesalers, retailers, and growers can interact and do business. CHEX, in particular, develops modern software and blockchain technology solutions to power business-to-business marketplaces. Moreover, their platform actually provides free market commerce, a rarity in the cannabis industry, which functions very much as a gray market because of the plant's designation as a schedule I drug.

Joining the cannatech revolution is as simple (and as complicated) as creating the next great website, app or data system to propel the industry forward. Programmers, coders, software designers, application developers and all other tech lovers have ample opportunity to make their moves in the industry.

51. If you are already working in the information technology sector, what type of services could you cross over into the cannabis industry?

52. Can you create and implement a technological process that helps solve some of the industry's challenges? If so, what would your technology resolve?

(Hint: think about the challenges outlined in this book!)

53. Can you transfer skills like human resources, IT, content creation, and compliance and carve a niche in this sector?

MARKETING:

Event Marketing
Content Marketing
Influencer Marketing

Like any industry, marketing is essential for cannabis businesses. Every enterprise must promote its products and services to potential consumers using a multichannel marketing matrix, including paid advertising, affiliate promotions, public relations and social media. This matrix development is a core component of any strategic marketing plan, whether targeting other businesses or individual consumers. Because cannabis is for the moment illegal on the federal level, marketing in the industry is more nuanced and proscribed than other sectors, which can often leaning in on more personal connections with the target market. Furthermore, a large portion of marketing will need to include re-education and possibly debunking myths or stereotypes surround cannabis.

54. With what you've learned so far, what are three ways you can use public relations and marketing skills to assist the cannabis industry globally?

Idea #1

Idea #2

Idea #3

Event Marketing

Advertising cannabis in traditionally mainstream outlets is currently very challenging and limited. **Event marketing** is perhaps the most prevalent form of marketing in the cannabis industry, particularly when it comes to the business to business (B2B) niche. Conferences like MJBizCon, Cannabis World Congress & Business Expo (CWCBE) and NECANN are designed to provide an industry overview, while events like IC3 are geared towards pairing investors with cannabis companies looking for capital. The Cannabis Science Conference, which occurs now on both east and west coasts, is one of the only conferences focused on cannabinoid research and technology. The event boasts some of the top cannabis scientists in the world and presentations for developing research ideas globally.

There are now cannabis conferences designed for almost every facet of the industry; information technology, the medical market and consumer education, including the Cannabis Education Advocacy Symposium & Expo (CEASE). CEASE is a consumer focused non-profit organization that I founded to educate our communities about the fact-based health and wellness benefits of the plant while highlighting the latest developments in state and federal legislation, social justice and business. The organization provides content and education on the local level across the country in partnership with the local municipality leaders, with audiences ranging from law enforcement to church attendees. Conversations are intimate and focused on the specific educational gaps of each community, regardless of legalization. While the

National Cannabis Festival attracts over 20,000 attendees every year for an annual policy summit and music festival celebration in Washington, D.C.

National Cannabis Festival 2019

Although new cannabis events popping up all the time, it is important that individuals interested in using events as a channel for marketing align with the target audience and overall intent or messaging of the event. I would also recommend multi-year or multi-event integrated partnerships to maximize return on investment. Use the first sponsorship or participation to test the waters, but if you have found a strong working relationship with the event's leadership, you will find the relationship and ROI can only be strengthened by an ongoing collaboration. In 2018, my company used the Women Grow Leadership Summit to relaunch The WeedHead™, sponsoring a memorable rest and recharge lounge for attendees to support my 2nd year presenting at the conference. As the year progressed, we went on to collaborate on multiple local Women Grow events in the NY, NJ and PA tri-state region to successfully capitalize on the national summit momentum and our company's tri-state roots. We were able to quickly build brand recognition and increase website traffic using this 6-month, highly focused event marketing strategy.

Content Marketing

Big cannabis brands crave traditional advertising channels and a number of media outlets, both digital and print have cropped up to close the gap. Some examples include High Times, one of the oldest cannabis publications, Honeysuckle, specifically aimed at women, and Cannabis Science & Technology, which focuses on new research in the industry. These strategic business partnerships with cannabis media outlets function very similarly to traditional media partnerships where brands have an option between cost per click banner ads, traditional print ads, or sponsored integrated content. In these scenarios, it is a best practice to utilize multiple levers across the outlet, but more and more **integrated content marketing** proves to be most cost effective for brand marketing budgets. This is particularly the case with clickbait topics that offer helpful insights for readers. Also called native advertising, this is a service usually offered by all media outlets but can be challenging to execute if the integrated content used doesn't align authentically with the brand's product and/or the content itself doesn't receive enough traffic to be meaningful.

ESTROHAZE   Leafly   HoneySuckle MAGAZINE

Some of the most recognizable and respected brands in the content marketing niche are service oriented digital platforms such as Leafly, Weedmaps and EstroHaze, a platform dedicated to connecting people of color to the cannabis movement. Creating a content platform is a relatively low-cost way to add your voice to the cannabis industry. An understanding of SEO, content curation and a regular posting schedule are necessities for launching and growing successful online platforms. Magazines and other print publications involve a higher level of investment, but custom publishers can help streamline those efforts.

Content is a powerful draw because stories teach us what it means to be human. Media created for cannabis has the potential to educate millions about the powers of plant medicine, dispelling myths and over 80 years of propaganda. There is a huge thirst for cannabis knowledge and re-education. Prohibition has led to decades of misinformation and stigma; as the legalization movement grows, so do the millions around the globe seeking the truth. Through strong content marketing, there is a tremendous opportunity to introduce people to the new faces of cannabis culture and enhance the knowledge and legitimacy of those already involved. Podcasts have become a legitimate online media outlet and not surprisingly, podcasts that focus specifically on the cannabis industry continue to emerge. She Blaze, a concept created by my sister Ice Dawson in 2017, is a frank and funny live weekly video podcast that highlights cannabis culture and business from a woman's point of view. Since launching, I have joined the cast as a co-host and our podcast has evolved to include integrated product placement and brand promotion with syndication on iHeartRadio, iTunes and Soundcloud. Despite the increase in popularity and engagement for video and audio content, the ability to write as a form of content is still important because all content eventually needs a little copy to support. Search engine optimization (SEO) is really important for creating strong titles for clicks and keyword relevance in a google or social media search. Above all, to be successful in content development, there must be consistent delivery of compelling topics. Whether you settle on a monthly cadence or bi-weekly, it needs to be consistent and reliable for your audience.

Influencer Marketing

Dollar for dollar, influencer marketing is one of the most effective ways to build and scale a brand online, boost consumer engagement, and raise overall awareness of a product or service. By tapping into a trendsetter's existing fan base, savvy entrepreneurs can turbocharge the growth of their businesses. The secret to success is establishing a win-win partnership that offers value to both parties. Regardless of industry, affiliate sales programs, paid sponsorships, co-promotions and in-kind donations are all ways to work with influencers to introduce brands to new audiences and generate new leads.

There is tremendous opportunity to both become cannabis influencers and to leverage existing platforms. Social media savvy individuals unafraid to openly support cannabis and share their experiences can amass thousands of followers. Similar to content marketing, the key is consistency, and using hashtags, keywords and trending topics on prominent channels like Facebook, Instagram and Twitter to join and create community. Working with existing influencers involves creating strategic alliances that make sense for both parties. Offering someone with a six figure following free swag in exchange for promotion is an affront, and a waste of your time. Treat these deals as you would any celebrity endorsement. Influencers are micro (and sometimes bonafide) celebrities who deserve and demand affiliate commissions, paid product placement and sponsorships. The good news is that there are influencers at every popularity level, so find the most popular and professional that your budget will allow. The most successful influencer marketing programs work with a range of personalities with both large and small platforms. Each deal should be unique to the influencer.

Cannabis influencers span all areas we've discussed in this book and can be an individual, group or business entity. Some are focused on a cannabis consumption lifestyle while others are simply outspoken advocacy pioneers. As mainstream interest and acceptance of cannabis grows, more personalities have publicly embraced the plant, particularly influencers from adjacent markets, such as music, entertainment and sports. People who'll wield true long-term influence in cannabis are likely those who consistently respect the plant and dispel myths, rather than feed into them. This is a significant and gradual shift from well-known, old school cannabis influencers that have focused mostly on partying and getting lit. Regardless of how you choose to be an influencer, the key to audience growth and sustainability is authenticity and consistent messaging.

55. What are some content or event marketing ideas to expand awareness about the industry and attract more consumers?

56. Are you a content creator and/or established blogger in another industry? How can you take your content creation skills and apply them to the cannabis industry?

57. Do you have previous brand marketing experience? If so, what are some ways to utilize this experience in the legal cannabis industry?

SALES AND DISTRIBUTION

Sales and distribution is essentially the system of moving cannabis from the point of production to the other parts of the supply chain, with the ultimate goal of getting it to the consumer. When we speak about sales in this chapter, we are primarily referencing business-to-business (B2B) sales within the cannabis supply chain en route to the final consumer. The first step is cannabis processing, which we discussed earlier in the workbook. Once the cannabis is processed and ready to be shipped, it must be transported from point A to point B. This can be handled in-house by a vertically integrated cannabis company or cannabis-focused distribution companies can satisfy that need, if the law permits.

For decades, moving hemp or marijuana have involved tremendous risk. Individuals distributing or transporting cannabis, more commonly known as drug trafficking, faced steeper penalties than small-time growers and local dealers. These types of businesses existed almost exclusively in the illegal, unregulated market However, as cannabis legalization continues to evolve, many companies are stepping into this necessary role especially as new adult-use markets open with distribution licensing as an option. Generally, distribution in the cannabis industry is a great white space to jump into the market. I would recommend looking at both hemp and marijuana opportunities. As you can expect, there are some common needs for companies operating in either space, but hemp is likely to be the faster route to successful revenue generation.

Distributors collect the cannabis from the cultivators and/or processors, and transport it to the manufacturers or directly to the dispensaries. Depending on the state and regulatory structure, some of these distributors actually purchase the cannabis and resell it to the next business in the supply chain, while others act solely as transportation resources charging fees for hauling the harvested plants. This is an emerging portion of the industry that is ripe for improvement through increased competition. If you are already in the business of highly regulated product distribution, like alcohol or cash, you are well positioned to cross over into the industry here. Moving cannabis often requires specialized vehicles and security. Although marijuana can only be distributed intrastate, subjecting young or harvested plants to long periods of ground transportation risks damaging the goods. Successful distributors generally start with at least one large vehicle equipped with a temperature control interior and possibly even built out to make packing and delivering plants, containers or bottles easier. In my time as an industry consultant, I have helped vet and secure cannabis distribution fleets for vertically integrated companies and often, it is much easier to sub-contract this to another company with distribution expertise. Some of these distribution companies further specialize in armed security and delivery to ensure the valuable merchandise, money or marijuana, reaches the final destination fully accounted for. For additional security, many vehicles will also have cameras installed to track activity both inside and outside of the van or truck.

The largest barrier to entry in this sector is licensing if required, and securing the vans or trucks that will be used for the work. In smaller markets, getting started might take just one van, but larger market entrants must contend with stronger competition. For example, some alcohol companies who have traditionally distributed wines and spirits are getting into the business and setting up new cannabis distribution entities. In fact, in the initial roll-out of adult-use legalization in Nevada, only alcohol distributors were awarded licenses to distribute cannabis. Also, some of the larger cannabis manufacturers have expanded their services and are distributing the products of their competitors alongside their own. Distribution-only companies are just starting to emerge within legal marijuana markets. This is an attractive entry point for people in legal markets with trucking or delivery experience and relationships with local growers and processors. That said, there is also an opportunity to do the same type of distribution work in hemp. Not only are the financial barriers to entry lower, those working in hemp can expand to multi-state operations because of hemp's legalized status.

In the early days of legalization, many states implemented vertically integrated models which initially gave licensing to very few businesses. In a vertically integrated model, licensed businesses are expected to do everything in the supply chain from seed to consumer sale. Under this model, there wasn't initially a need for strong sales executives, as most cultivators supplied their own dispensaries. To add diversity and stability to emerging markets, many states now allow multiple license types and varying business sizes across the supply chain, offering more competition for products at retail. For that reason, business-to-business (B2B) sales strategy and execution is now an integral part of getting different types of products to consumers at retail.

There are quite a few distribution companies that also include sales support in their suite of services or for their own in-house needs. Distribution is a huge growth sector in the industry, generating the most new jobs of any category. Big cannabis brands look to hire "brand ambassadors" or sales executives to represent the brand in the market selling to the retail dispensary buyers, usually the store managers. Similar to mainstream retail, success in the sales vertical is largely about relationship management. Top sales people in cannabis have usually had previous experience within the dispensary or at the cultivation. They either know where to source good product or to whom to sell, much like a broker. Individuals with previous pharmaceutical sales experience will certainly have an advantage crossing over into corporate cannabis sales positions. However, this sector is largely reserved for well-connected individuals.

If you are interested in pursuing sales opportunities in the legal cannabis industry, you must become part of the local community in the region you want to operate. For example, if you are anticipating a new market where you currently live, my recommendation is that you embrace local advocacy. Relationships in emerging markets are forged in the advocacy community. Out the gate, you will have a competitive advantage if you cultivate relationships with potential dispensary owners and other cannabis businesses in a developing market *before* the market opens. Sales executives can cover selling raw materials from cultivator to manufacturers or selling manufactured cannabis goods to dispensaries. A working knowledge of the important sales aspects of cannabis products will be important. From cannabinoid potency, to brand recognition, to new product opportunities, individuals in this sector need to truly be the product assortment experts, particularly as it pertains to the category being sold. While many markets will have sales executives that cover all range of products, larger markets are seeing separation of the market and salesforce by product type.

In the earliest legalized states, regulators misstepped by limiting the ability for strong sales and distribution verticals. For example, when Nevada only allowed cannabis distribution licenses to alcohol distribution companies, the state soon felt the strain of inexperienced distributors with limited bandwidth to support both alcohol and cannabis movement in Nevada. In 2018, within a month of opening a legal market with lines wrapped around the corner, Las Vegas dispensaries reported major cannabis flower shortages. In California, where only mega brands withstood the regulatory requirements of the new adult-use market, they soon realized it was necessary to start quickly expanding sales teams to support multiple regions versus in prior years when well-known brands were largely confined to one region. Whether you are in sales or distribution, the middle man of the cannabis supply chain is crucial to the success of any legal market.

58. Are you in sales? How can you transfer that skill to the cannabis industry?

59. As you in transportation or logistics? If so, how could you transfer that skill or your current capabilities into the cannabis industry?

60. What other ancillary skill or resource can you bring into the cannabis industry?

RETAIL

Retail operations represent the direct-to-consumer (DTC) portion of the cannabis industry. This is the part of the industry we are most familiar with and is considered the "sexy" part of the industry. Commonly referred to as a dispensary, cannabis retail stores sell flower and other products over the counter to both medical and adult-use consumers. Depending on the market, many dispensaries serve both consumer populations, offering lower prices and/or reduced taxes for consumers registered with the state as medical card holders. Brick and mortar dispensaries are the most visible part of the marijuana retail sector. While, hemp and hemp-derived CBD products are being sold frequently online via marketplaces and exchanges.

There are many different emerging retail models within the cannabis industry, from craft herbal apothecaries to big box retail experiences. There are farm-to-table models, where companies source cannabis directly from growers and deliver it straight to the consumer's home. For people who want to choose their own products and explore them in person, there are now dispensaries that offer attractive visual displays and even on-site consumption. This opportunity varies by market with some states, like Nevada, making on-site consumption at dispensaries illegal. While in California's Bay Area, there are a number of well-known dispensaries that offer an area or lounge for on-site consumption. Delivery companies also work independently with multiple dispensaries or as an extension of a singular dispensary license, adding an additional level of convenience and customer service to retail storefronts. Cannabis home delivery has grown tremendously as mainstream consumption increases. In some states, innovation from the legal market has infiltrated the illegal market as well. One of the biggest additions to the market for delivery has been integration of retail menus with phone applications, making service very on-demand for the consumer. A few distribution companies also play in the delivery space, capitalizing on access to vehicles and drivers. However, by and large, the type of scale required for B2B distribution versus business-to-consumer (B2C) delivery varies widely. For example, retail products can be transported in a personal vehicle.

Subscription boxes are also a retail option growing in popularity as more users embrace trying cannabis again or for the first time. Most subscription services like Hemper and 420 Goodybox contain cannabis related accessories to support a consumer's lifestyle. This includes rolling papers, trays, grinders and containers. Federal legalization of hemp has expanded retail experiences to include subscription models as well. Hello Jane is an example of a hemp-based CBD subscription box, similar to Birch Box, for individuals looking to try new and reliable CBD products on the market. I believe that soon, we'll see subscription boxes that actually contain marijuana, particularly in states that allow adult use.

61. Are you already delivery or Uber/Lyft driver in a market where cannabis delivery is possible? Do you already have a network of clients or consumers interested in buying cannabis products? What steps would you need to take to establish a cannabis delivery business?

62. Do you have a retail space or any business/practice with a retail component that you can add products that include cannabis?

Hint: these can also be hemp-derived products, which are subject to few regulations

63. What other steps can you take to enter the retail space in your current market? What are some ideas that will make your store experience unique?

TOURISM

Adult-use legalization has created a booming market for cannabis tourism in the United States and abroad. People from cannabis-prohibited areas are flocking to places with legal access to consume cannabis and experience the local culture. Additionally, as cannabis becomes more accepted for its health and wellness properties, there will be more and more medical consumers that are looking for accommodations for access and/or treatment. Like any other tourists, they want to sample the local scene, which includes touring dispensaries, farms and other cannabis themed destinations. They are going to want to see all facets of the local cannabis community, including manufacturing as well as where and how locals consume.

There is massive potential for tourism in adult-use friendly areas. Think of it like tourism in wine countries. Those tourists will need cannabis friendly accommodations, a stark contrast to the hotels where tourists are required to pay hefty penalties if they consume in their rooms. There is a huge opportunity to capitalize on tourism by creating accommodations without draconian restrictions for cannabis users.

Bud & Bougie Denver 2018 - (L-to-R) The Dank Duchess, David Kellman, Tanganyika "Tangy' Daniels

There are also vaporizer rental services available in Denver, which are ideal for visitors unwilling to spend upwards of $500 on devices that they cannot use at home. Cannabis concierge consultants, like Tanganyika Daniels of Jayn Green who specializes in international cannabis tourism, help curate the cannabis experiences for out-of-towners and busy locals. They function as personal guides, introducing tourists and guests to the area's cannabis education, community and culture. While opening up cannabis friendly hotels may be prohibitively expensive for many would-be entrepreneurs, there is a place in the tourism industry for everyone. Starting a cannabis themed tour or opening up a concierge business is as simple as getting to know your local industry and its players, and creating a compelling digital presence--website, social media platforms etc. You can build a fun, exciting and profitable business based on local goods and services. When it comes to figuring out a role in the blossoming cannabis tourism industry, the only limit is your imagination.

64. Can you turn your passion for meeting new people into a business? Do you already have a travel agency business? If so, what can you offer in the cannabis tourism sector?

65. What tools can you use to create a distinctive cannabis themed experience for others in your home state?

66. Do you have a space to create a one of a kind cannabis experience for people curious about trying cannabis again or for the first time?

EVENTS

Providing education and empowerment can happen in numerous ways, such as events offering people face-to-face contact with advocates, innovators and positive experiences in controlled settings. There was a time when bringing together too many cannabis consumers in one place might trigger a police raid. Now, there are safe spaces to celebrate cannabis culture and enjoy the incredible creativity and connection that comes from the plant, and fellowship with other cannabis consumers. As cannabis increases in popularity, we are seeing the plant infused into experiences such as weddings or corporate events. No longer do we have to expect a sesh to be in a poorly lit, dungeon-like venue. From infused menus designed by top chefs, such as Executive Chef Scott Durrah, to intimate consumption re-education with companies like Topshelf Budtending, the sky's the limit for cannabis events. If you are already an event coordinator or promoter, this might be one of the best ways to cross over into the industry adding your expertise for decor, vendors and logistics to the industry.

67. Name some different types of events that you can use to promote cannabis. How would you provide attendees with an unforgettable experience?

68. Do your skills involve party planning? How can you create a premium cannabis consumption experience?

69. What are some ways to bring cooking or entertainment skills into the cannabis industry?

Bud & Bougie Denver 2018; Andrew Mieure, Founder of Topshelf Budtending

REAL ESTATE

We've covered all of the categories dealing directly with the plant, but the following ancillary markets are in some ways just as critical. Properly zoned real estate is essential for getting into any facet of the cannabis business. And, there are companies designed to help cannabis businesses identify and develop real estate. Their services run the gamut from purchasing real estate on behalf of cannabis companies and leasing it back to developing properties to providing financing for build out and development. Not to mention architects and contracting firms with the expertise to design and manage construction.

Real estate professionals can come into the cannabis industry and specialize in any of those particular areas. In fact, almost every skill set has a counterpart in cannabis. The industry is actively seeking people in real estate and there are significant premiums for working in the space. Seasoned real estate professionals can deploy their current skills and contacts to reap significant gains. However, entering the cannabis real estate market is not without risk.

There is speculative risk, but that is normal for all real-estate transactions. However, there is one major risk you assume in cannabis, albeit slight, and that is civil forfeiture, the federal government's right to seize any property being used for cannabis because it remains a schedule I drug. The probability of a civil forfeiture is low because of rare bipartisan support for banning the DEA from using federal forfeiture funds in its war on drugs. The current administration has also testified in front of Congress, promising not to conduct these types of seizures. However, until a ban is codified into law, the risk, though slight, remains.

70. Are you in finance? How can you transfer that skill to the cannabis industry?

71. How can you transfer real estate services to the cannabis industry? Can you lease property? Can you assist in finding property?

72. What other ancillary skill or resource can you bring into the cannabis industry?

INSURANCE

As the cannabis industry matures, the need and accessibility of insurance to manage some of the related risks also grows. This is especially true when high level investors become involved in cannabis projects. The investors want assurances that in the event of a bad crop, a worker's slip and fall judgment, or criminal activity and acts of God, that some portion of their investments can be recouped.

When the industry began, insurance companies assiduously avoided cannabis. However, as the cannabis movement gains popularity and momentum, companies willing to work with industry businesses have come forward to offer insurance for a range of activities.

73. What are some insurance services that you can provide for cannabis businesses or their owners?

74. Can you provide consulting advice for start-up cannabis businesses in the insurance sector? Name 2-3 key pieces of information that you think might be valuable.

75. What should be included in insurance plans tailored to the cannabis industry to address the current challenges, gaps and concerns?

HUMAN RESOURCES

Human resources and management is another one of those basic services that must be provided in order for the industry to stabilize and operate like more traditional sectors such as banking or healthcare.

1. Recruiting
2. Training
3. Payroll processing
4. Employee Relations

Every company with more than one employee will need human resources support for recruiting, training, payroll and benefits, and employee relations. Companies like Wurk now provide a full suite of outsourced HR services to cannabis businesses, while others like Vangst and THC Staffing focus on recruiting. HR professionals looking to enter the industry can start businesses as consultants, which still offers tremendous opportunity for growth. Alternately, there are opportunities in human resources roles at established cannabis companies.

76. List three ways to provide unique services in the human resources sector.

Idea #1

Idea #2

Idea #3

LEGAL

The cannabis industry was created and is governed by laws and countless regulations. Therefore, attorneys and compliance officers are essential to the industry's growth and success. Opportunities exist in every specialty, from real estate to regulatory law, to government relations and criminal law. The need for qualified legal professionals is almost inexhaustible. Lawyers practicing in legalized states can brush up on the current law, and in many cases jump right into the industry. As someone with experience working in partnership with legal experts, I find intellectual property protections and employment/labor law with respect to cannabis to be particularly important. Frankly, as long as cannabis is federally illegal, there will be a need for criminal lawyers in the industry.

77. How can you transfer your legal skills to the cannabis sector?

78. Can you create contracts to help cannabis businesses, or help broker deals between companies?

79. How can you get involved to advocate for legal change in the cannabis industry?

EDUCATION

Though I briefly touched on education earlier, it is so important that I must expound. Cannabis isn't just an industry, it's a movement. Knowledge is the most critical step to ensuring that all people have access to the plant's wellness benefits. **Qualified educators** and education are paramount to the industry's continued growth and development. Consumers need education about the plant and available products, the best way to purchase them, and fair pricing. Entrepreneurs and prospective employees need training on basic business practices, as well as industry regulations and specific cannabis related knowledge. There is currently a huge shortage of training programs for cannabis employees, with Oaksterdam as one of the few nationally-recognized cannabis educational institutions.

Many state regulations now mandate employee-training courses, all but guaranteeing a built-in market for corporate education. Fortunately, there is still opportunity to capitalize on this white space. For example, Elevated Education LLC, a women and minority-owned cannabis education company, is an Illinois state-certified responsible vendor training partner. The company provides cannabis operators the training required by the state for cannabis business licensing and renewal. Barriers to entry are much lower than plant-touching cannabis operations. It is important to educate yourself prior to entering the market. The most comprehensive options involve certification by education platforms in more established markets. Nothing is worse than claiming to be an expert and providing misinformation. Use caution when sharing educational information that you have not created or verified. The ability to develop curriculum and viable course materials will give individuals a competitive advantage entering this sector.

In addition to educating cannabis operators, budtenders and patients, there are also lucrative opportunities to educate professionals like lawyers, doctors and other professionals required to take continuing education courses to maintain licenses or certification. As cannabis gains popularity, many professionals will elect continuing education coursework in cannabis to learn more about the plant and the industry. After all, if you were a tax professional and had a choice to take a course, would you choose the latest arcane IRS regulations regarding depreciation, or a class on cannabis and taxes? For example, Cansoom is an educational business started by a nurse practitioner. The company provide cannabis education to licensed health professionals ultimately certifying them as a Medical Cannabis Consultant™. Cansoom has quickly grown into a global network of licensed health professionals competent in cannabis as medicine.

80. Do you have experience as a teacher or corporate trainer? If so, how might you offer your expertise to the legal cannabis industry?

81. Are you a conscious cannabis consumer with knowledge about the cannabis products in your market? How might you use this knowhow to educate other consumers? What are key tools needed to get started?

82. Are you a health professional with an understanding of the endocannabinoid system? How could you use education as a means to create revenue?

PART 2:
Key Takeaways

The biggest takeaway from the second half of this workbook is that the cannabis industry is like a glacier, quite large and far reaching. What you have learned in this book is simply the tip of the iceberg. However, I hope you take these seeds of information and plant them in your own garden. There is cannabis wealth being generated by individuals who are already privileged with access to capital and other important resources. While I don't fault anyone willing to take the risk to pursue opportunities in this developing industry, it is important to acknowledge that countless individuals have already suffered greatly in the prohibition of cannabis. As the world finally learns about cannabis and its value, it is only fair that the harms inflicted by prohibition globally on vulnerable communities be rectified. Certainly, the government has a responsibility to implement cannabis laws, regulations and policies rooted in justice, equity and inclusion. Yet, it is just as important that motivated members of these same communities smartly step up to create opportunities and strategy will be important to navigate this burgeoning industry, quickly filling with suits and sharks. Equity programs are a good start, but truly leveling the playing field requires education and empowerment for those already facing tremendous disadvantages. This was a key motivation for our company's decision to publish this workbook series. There are no shortcuts in the cannabis business, but a thorough understanding of industry dynamics coupled with a pragmatic approach to providing value to the industry based upon one's existing skill set can propel people to success, even without six-figure start-up capital or high-level connections.

To support your continued cannabis journey and help you develop a personalized plan for success, here are a few additional takeaways from Part 2:

- **Think about hemp first.** If you can imagine your business idea on the marijuana side, spend some time strategizing that same idea in hemp. You'd be pleasantly surprised at how much further your business plan can go with a different regulatory structure. You will still earn experience in the cannabis industry and develop relationships with potential strategic partners for when you're in a position to launch a marjuana focused business. The cannabis industry is quickly converging as real science is reveals the connection between marijuana and hemp.

- **Use your credentials and experience.** So many people want to jump into cannabis but limit their research to only the sexy sectors, usually touching the plant. However, using your experience and credentials in an ancillary approach is a much faster route to revenue generation in the cannabis industry. Your positive contributions to the market will be far greater if you start with an area in which you have verified expertise.

- **Dispel myths rather than perpetuate them.** Everyone has heard their share of stereotypical jokes about cannabis users and the "budding" industry. However, once you decide to build a legitimate business within the legal market and increase your education, it is important that you actively work to debunk common myths. This includes not perpetuating old beliefs or leaning into those stereotypes in marketing, public relations and media.

CONCLUSION:
Join the Cannabis Community

Cannabis isn't the next big thing, it is now officially 'the thing'. It's the first new industry in the United States in a generation, and in five short years since Colorado became the first state to completely abolish prohibition, America's cannabis industry has mushroomed to an estimated $10 billion dollars annually, with continued double digit growth on the horizon. This is only the beginning. As more states legalize and more consumers join the movement, entrepreneurs who've founded businesses and people who cross over their skills into the industry today will be positioned to profit off of growing demand tomorrow.

If you are even remotely interested in the cannabis industry, take the leap to establish your business in the market. Educate yourself about the plant, and its history. Expand on the foundation that has been provided by this book. Take classes, like our cannabis introductory course, attend business conferences, join advocacy associations, and read everything you can get your hands on. Think about your passions, skills and talents and how you can best apply them to a rapidly evolving market.

Opportunities like these don't come around very often and you owe it to yourself to fully explore this one. When I took the leap years ago, I had no idea what the future would hold. I believed in myself and the importance of making the plant and the industry accessible to all people and communities, particularly those like the one I grew up, which has been destroyed by America's war on drugs. It's been a whirlwind as a cannapreneur, filled with non-THC induced dizzying highs and lows, and even a brush with law enforcement. But, I have absolutely no regrets about my journey. I hope that you will connect with our team on social media and join our online learning portal, MJM Learn™. Together, we can forge a brighter and more inclusive future for the cannabis community. Together, we can change the world.

83. How can you start as an entrepreneur in this industry?

84. What are some ways that you can create cannabis projects or gain employment or experience in the cannabis industry?

85. How can you enter into the industry in compliance with your current state laws? What are some ways you can assist with regulations in your state?

15 PRACTICE QUESTIONS:
Test Your Cannabis Knowledge

86. What are the major differences between marijuana and hemp? Name at least 3.

87. List at least 3 commonly found molecular components of all cannabis plants?

88. What are the main sectors of the cannabis industry that are considered "plant-touching"? What are some of the risks associated with entering the market through these sectors?

89. What are the main sectors of the cannabis industry that are considered "plant-touching"? What are some of the risks with entering the market through these sectors?

90. What is the difference between medical cannabis and adult-use cannabis?

91. Who are the top organizations advocating for cannabis legalization globally? Name at least 3.

92. What are the most common methods of cannabis extraction? Name and describe at least 3.

93. What is the major difference between solvent-LESS and solvent-FREE extraction methods?

94. Name at least 4 types of cannabis concentrate outside of oil or tincture?

95. Why was cannabis prohibited and criminalized in the United States during the 1940s?

96. What are some of the top roles available in the cannabis industry?

97. What are the federal bills for hemp and marijuana that dictate legalization? What does it mean to be Schedule I?

98. Name the core parts of the cannabis plant and key differences among the parts.

Hint: Go back to the Hemp chapter

99. What are the different types of infused cannabis products on the market? What are key differences with onset and bioavailability for these different types?

100. How many grams are in an ounce of cannabis? How many grams are in an eighth of cannabis?

WHERE IN THE WORLD IS THE WEEDHEAD™?

For more education, empowerment & equity opportunities, follow The WeedHead™ & Company!

Website: www.theweedhead.com

Facebook: www.fb.com/theweedheadco

Instagram: @TheWeedHeadCo

Twitter: @TheWeedHeadCo

Youtube: www.youtube.com/theweedhead

—

Catch up with Dasheeda Dawson, The WeedHead™ on multiple platforms:

Facebook: www.fb.com/theweedhead

Instagram: @TheCannabisCEO

Twitter: @TheCannabisCEO

—

We put our years of cannabis and business experience in one convenient education and learning portal. Join MJM Learn™, the higher community!

Website: www.theweedhead.com/mjm-learn

Facebook: www.fb.com/mjmlearn

FB Group: www.fb.com/groups/mjmlearn

She Blaze is a trailblazing Zoomcast bringing cannabis culture from a woman's perspective to the mainstream. Co-hosts Dasheeda and Ice are millennial women offering a frank and funny take on the industry, combining keen business insight with head-nodding real talk, news, reviews, and interviews. **Welcome to a bold new take on the high life!**

SHE BLAZE

The 30-min long weekly show offers a glimpse into life of trendsetting thought-leader Dasheeda Dawson, with 'Where in the World is The WeedHead™' and the fun, girly, cultural intersection with little sister, Ice Dawson, the Cannabis Socialite whose bubbly personality and striking white ensembles have made her a rising influencer on the cannabis social scene. Dasheeda is an internationally renowned cannabis leader and expert who has used her business acumen and background in molecular biology to shape multi-million dollar industry projects. While Ice isn't just the life of the party, she also knows how to get it started as an event producer. Together, they offer an incisive industry perspective fueled by their on-the-ground experience. **Join them on *iHeartRadio, Soundcloud* and *Facebook* every Saturday at 11am EST for the latest from the world of cannabis.**

MINORITIES FOR MEDICAL MARIJUANA (M4MM)

Minorities for Medical Marijuana Inc. is a 501c3 non-profit organization focused on providing cannabis advocacy, education, outreach and training to communities of color throughout the country. The cornerstone of its mission is fostering inclusive and equitable cannabis public policy, healthcare awareness, business development, and social reform. The organization is committed to cultivating a culturally inclusive environment where diversity of thought, experience, and opportunities are valued, respected, appreciated and celebrated. Currently, M4MM has a presence in 27 states throughout the country and was awarded 2018 Cannabis Industry Organization of the Year designation by Cannabis Business Awards.

Join the M4MM network at www.M4MMUnited.org

c.e.a.s.e. — CANNABIS EDUCATION ADVOCACY SYMPOSIUM & EXPO

Cannabis Education Advocacy Symposium & Expo (CEASE) is a 501c3 nonprofit organization with a mission to promote inclusion, equity and justice in the cannabis community by increasing awareness and educating consumers, particularly those marginalized by prohibition, about the medical and economic benefits of the plant. Globally, the organization looks to cease misconceptions and to enhance consumer understanding by providing a strong platform for informed cannabis industry thought leadership, innovative brand exhibition and education on the evolution of the cannabis plant across health/wellness, policy advocacy and business.

Learn more at www.CEASEconference.org

Brand Credits and Acknowledgement

All logos and images highlighted in this book are the ownership of brands and companies listed below.

Minorities For Medical Marijuana PG **1-4, 44, 150**, Bud & Bougie PG **3**, Beverly Gray Business Exchange Center PG **4**, Target Corporation PG **11-14**, Victoria's Secret PG **13**, MJM Strategy PG **15**, Levi Strauss PG **24-26**, Harborside Health Center PG **32**, Discovery Channel's "Weed Wars" PG **32**, The Pot Book (Dr. Julie Holland) PG **35**, ABCs of CBD (Shira Adler) PG **35**, Vitamin Weed (Dr. Michele Ross) PG **35**, Start Your Own Cannabis Business (Javier Hasse) PG **35**, NORML PG **36**, Women Grow PG **36**, Cannagather PG **36**, Symbiotic Genetics PG **42**, Sensi Seeds PG **43**, Exoticgeniccs PG **43**, Crockett Family Farms PG **43**, Dark Heart Nursery PG **43, 45**, Jungle Boys PG **45, 53**, Steephill Labs (Dr. Reggie Gaudino) PG **46**, NY State Senator James Sanders PG **49**, Wonderland Farms PG **50**, Swami™ Select PG **52**, Marigold™ California PG **52**, Honeydew Farms PG **52**, LiveWell™ Colorado PG **53**, Ten Four Farms PG **53**, Clean Green Certified™ (Chris Van Hook) PG **54**, The Dank Duchess PG **59, 107, 120**, BAS Research PG **61**, Moxie PG **64**, Blue River Terps™ PG **64**, Cresco Cannabis extract types PG **64**, Wana Brands PG **66**, Dixie™ Elixirs PG **66**, Kiva™ Confections PG **66**, Mary's Medicinals™ PG **66, 71**, Prana PG **67, 75**, CannaStrips™ PG **71**, 1906 PG **75**, ViPova™ Tea PG **75**, PuffCo PG **77**, Ardent PG **77**, Volcano Vaporizer PG **77**, CCELL Technology PG **79**, The Blinc Group (Arnaud Dumas de Rauly) PG **79**, Marijuana Tax Act PG **82**, Hemp Farming Act of 2018 PG **83**, Canopy Growth PG **84**, New Frontier Data PG **85**, Hemp Industry Journal PG **86**, Charlotte's Web PG **86**, Holmes Organics PG **88**, Erbanna PG **95**, Kushco Holdings PG **96**, StartSMART Coalition PG **98**, CannaTrax (C-Trax) PG **99**, Jade Insights PG **99**, Cannabis Hemp Exchange PG **99**, National Cannabis Festival (NCF) PG **104**, Cannabis World Congress & Business Expo (CWCBExpo) PG **104**, NECANN PG **104**, Cannabis Education Advocacy Symposium & Expo (CEASE) PG **104-105, 150**, NYC Cannabis Parade PG **104**, EstroHaze PG **106**, Leafly PG **106**, Honeysuckle Magazine PG **106**, Weedmaps PG **106**, She Blaze PG **107, 149**, Jodie Emery PG **108**, Sonia Gomez PG **108**, Jayn Green (Tangyanika Daniels) PG **120**, Scott Durrah PG **122**, Topshelf Budtending (Andrew Mieure) PG **122-124**, Vangst PG **130**, THC Staffing PG **130**, Oaksterdam University PG **134**, Elevated Education LLC (Kiana Hughes) PG **134**, Cansoom (Lolita Kornegay) PG **135**

CPSIA information can be obtained
at www.ICGtesting.com
Printed in the USA
LVHW021707150521
687406LV00001B/19